Argumentation
Analysis, Evaluation, Presentation

Additional LEA titles in Argumentation include

van Eemeren et al. • *Fundamentals of Argumentation Theory: A Handbook of Historical Backgrounds and Contemporary Developments*

Johnson • *Manifest Rationality: A Pragmatic Theory of Argument*

van Eemeren and Grootendorst • *Argumentation, Communication, and Fallacies: A Pragma-Dialectical Perspective*

For additional information, contact Lawrence Erlbaum Associates, Inc., or view the online catalog at *www.erlbaum.com*.

Argumentation
Analysis, Evaluation, Presentation

Frans H. van Eemeren
Rob Grootendorst
A. Francisca Snoeck Henkemans

LEA
LAWRENCE ERLBAUM ASSOCIATES, PUBLISHERS
2002   Mahwah, New Jersey   London

Lawrence Erlbaum Associates, Inc., Publishers
10 Industrial Avenue
Mahwah, NJ 07430

Cover design by Kathryn Houghtaling Lacey

Library of Congress Cataloging-in-Publication Data

Eemeren, F. H. van.
Argumentation : analysis, evaluation, presentation / Frans H. van Eemeren, Rob Grootendorst, A. Francisca Snoeck Henkemans.
    p. cm.
Includes bibliographical references and index.
ISBN 0-8058-3952-6 (pbk. : alk. paper)
1. Persuasion (Rhetoric)   I. Grootendorst, R.   II. Snoeck Henkemans, A. F.   III. Title.
P301 .5.P47 E327   2001
808—dc21   2001040403
                                                                   CIP

Books published by Lawrence Erlbaum Associates are printed on acid-free paper, and their bindings are chosen for strength and durability.

Printed in the United States of America
10   9   8   7   6   5   4   3   2

Contents

vi *CONTENTS*

II: EVALUATION

Preface

*A*rgumentation is an introduction to analyzing, evaluating, and presenting oral and written argumentation. It is based on a series of basic insights from the *pragma-dialectical* theory of argumentation. In this theory, argumentation is viewed as primarily aimed at resolving a difference of opinion by verbal means. As a consequence, argumentation is examined as part of an explicit or (in case of a monologue) implicit discussion between two parties that have different positions with respect to the same proposition. Each party's argumentation is directed at ending the difference by convincing the other party of the acceptability of a certain standpoint.

Argumentation deals with the identification of differences of opinion, the determination of unexpressed premises, the exposition of argument schemes, the analysis of the structure of argumentation, the evaluation of the soundness of argumentation, and the detection of fallacies as violations of rules for critical discussion. To cater for the needs of a large group of learners, the oral and written presentations of argumentation are also explicitly addressed. The material that is to be explained is divided into 10 separate chapters. Each of the chapters begins with a brief summary of its essentials, and closes with some suggestions for further reading (including other approaches), and a number of carefully selected exercises. Where this is due, some special assignments are added which can be used by the students and the instructor to test the progress the students have made in mastering the skills related to the preceding chapters.

Argumentation is a textbook based on earlier drafts that were for several years used in several universities in several countries. In various respects, *Argumentation* is not the traditional kind of textbook in its traditional format. *Argumentation* primarily aims at getting its readers interested in reflecting on the characteristics and peculiarities of argumentation—as it occurs in practice—by systematically providing readers with the basic conceptual framework and terminology for doing so. The book is meant to be a useful and inspiring starting point for those people interested in studying argumentation. We therefore strongly encourage all of its users, teachers and students alike, to let us know where they think something in the book is wrong or, as the case might be, alright.

Argumentation is, much to our regret, published after the untimely death of our co-author Rob Grootendorst. It goes without saying that we missed him in many ways when completing the manuscript. Fortunately, our friends in the international community of argumentation scholars and our colleagues in the Department of Speech Communication, Argumentation Theory, and Rhetoric of the University of Amsterdam have supported us in every way they could. We are particularly grateful to our North American colleagues Hans Hansen, Scott Jacobs, and Leah Polcar, who, during their visits to Amsterdam, contributed a great deal to the improvement of this book. Professor Erik Krabbe sent us, as always, his pertinent and detailed remarks from Groningen, which are, as always, highly appreciated. Last but not least, we thank Bart Garssen, Peter Houtlosser, Agnès van Rees, Maarten van der Tol, and all the students who took part in our argumentation courses at the University of Amsterdam and Utrecht University College for their helpful comments.

—*Frans H. van Eemeren*
—*A. Francisca Snoeck Henkemans*

Introduction

*T*his book treats argumentation as a means of resolving a difference of opinion. Not only in everyone's private life do differences of opinion constantly emerge in contacts with other people, but also at work and in all areas of public life. Sometimes the differences pertain to important matters and sometimes they are rather trivial. They can just as well manifest themselves in a conversation or at a meeting as in an essay or a written response to something read in a newspaper. In all these cases, advancing argumentation is a reasonable way of trying to put the difference of opinion to an end. Advancing argumentation means that the speaker or writer engages in a discussion with those who do not agree with his or her standpoint. Such argumentative discussions are pivotal to social life.

Argumentation is a verbal activity that can be performed orally as well as in writing. It is also a social activity: In advancing argumentation, one directs oneself by definition to others. In addition, argumentation is a rational activity that is aimed at defending a standpoint in such a way that it becomes acceptable to a critic who takes a reasonable attitude. By advancing argumentation, the speaker or writer starts from the—correct or wrong—assumption that there is a difference of opinion between him or her and the listener or reader. By putting forward propositions that must justify the standpoint at issue, the speaker or writer attempts to convince the listener or reader of the acceptability of this standpoint. The following definition of argumentation combines these various features:

Argumentation is a verbal, social, and rational activity aimed at convincing a reasonable critic of the acceptability of a standpoint by putting forward a constellation of one or more propositions to justify this standpoint.

This definition does not only refer to the activity of advancing arguments but also to the shorter or longer text that results from it. Argumentation relates both to the process of putting forward argumentation and to its "product," and the term *argumentation* covers the two of them. In argumentation theory, argumentation is viewed not only as the product of a rational process of reasoning, like arguments are traditionally seen in logic, but also as part of a developing communication and interaction process.

In a purely logical approach to argumentation, a great number of verbal, contextual, situational, and other pragmatic factors that affect the conduct and the outcome of an argumentative exchange are not regarded. In precisely what way are the arguments phrased? To whom are they in fact directed? In what kind of situation has the argumentation been advanced? What information conveyed by the utterances that precede the argumentation needs to be taken into account? Logicians are generally not concerned with these and other "pragmatic" questions. Rather, they concentrate on abstract "argument forms" or "patterns of reasoning," put in a standard formulation, in which a conclusion is derived from a certain set of premises. The main point for logicians is how to distinguish between "formally valid" argument forms and argument forms that are not formally valid. In order to be able to do so, they abstract from pragmatic properties of the argumentative reality that are indispensable for an adequate treatment of argumentation. In argumentation theory, on the contrary, the center of attention is the argumentation in actual practice, advanced by someone who tries to convince someone else of the acceptability of a certain standpoint.

People who make use of argumentation always appeal—whether explicitly or implicitly—to some standard of reasonableness. This, however, does not always mean that each argumentation is indeed reasonable. Argumentation in ordinary practice often appears to suffer from all kinds of defects. It is one of the aims of the study of argumentation to develop the tools for determining to what extent an argumentation is in agreement with the norms for a reasonable discussion. In this sense, argumentation theory has a *normative* dimension. It also has a *descriptive* dimension, for the technical notions that are employed in argumentation theory are closely related to the way argumentative discourse is conducted in argumentative reality and to the practical problems that may occur. In the method for analyzing, evaluating, and presenting argumentation that is introduced in this book, these two dimensions are systematically integrated.

We begin our treatment of argumentation theory at the same juncture where argumentation also starts in practice: the difference of opinion that occasions the evolvement of the argumentation. In chapter 1 and chapter 2, all terms and concepts are introduced that are of importance to the identification of differences of opinion. It is also clearly indicated which types of differences of opinion are to be distinguished. In order to explain that a difference of opinion can only be really resolved with the help of an argumentative discussion that is in agreement with certain preconditions, a model is presented of the various stages an argumentative discussion must ideally go through and whose main constituent is the argumentation proper.

Without a clear view of the difference of opinion around which the argumentation centers, an adequate analysis of the argumentation cannot possibly be given, but it goes without saying that the analysis is much more encompassing. It is, for instance, necessary to determine in a well-considered way exactly which arguments are explicitly or implicitly adduced and what should happen in case it is not entirely clear whether or not a certain part of the discourse is to be considered argumentative. All this is explained in chapter 3. In particular, for detecting unexpressed elements in the argumentation, it is helpful to have an understanding of the rules that are normally observed in ordinary communication. Indirect forms of argumentation and unexpressed standpoints can then be more easily identified. Chapter 4 provides the information required for these purposes. It is also essential to make an analysis of the advanced argumentation, which displays its argumentation structure. Chapter 5 provides the means for doing this.

In its turn, the analysis of the argumentation is the point of departure for the evaluation. In chapter 6, the various aspects of the evaluation of argumentation are discussed. Special attention is given to the different kinds of argument schemes that are used in argumentative practice to defend a standpoint. Each scheme involves the need to ask certain critical questions. In chapter 7 and chapter 8, ten rules for conducting a reasonable argumentative discussion are discussed, and fallacies that occur if a rule is violated are identified. Besides examples of violations of the rules, the technical names of the fallacies are provided.

Chapters 9 and 10 deal with the presentation of argumentation in a text or a speech. In this endeavor, the various kinds of insight that are acquired when dealing with the identification of differences of opinion and the analysis and evaluation of argumentation are an indispensable starting point. First, attention is paid to written argumentation, then to oral argumentation. In writing or rewriting an argumentative text, the analytic overview of the argumentative text, made with the help of the understanding gained earlier, is an excellent point of departure. The treatment of the oral argumentative speech concentrates on students' participation in an argumentative discussion and their preparation and presentation of a complete argumentative speech.

The method that is followed in this book is to teach step by step the insights that are required to perform the different tasks that have to be carried out well to analyze, evaluate, and present argumentation adequately and to be able to reflect on the problems that may be encountered. After each chapter, a number of exercises are included that students can use to master the material. Also, there are references to other theoretical literature. A short summary of the essentials can be found at the beginning of each chapter. Where it seems most suitable, more extensive exercises are added that pertain to a variety of aspects of the material previously treated. A detailed index can be found at the end of the book. This index is preceded by a list of the discussion rules, the fallacies, and a series of general references.

I

Analysis

1

Differences of Opinion

A n analysis of argumentation must begin by identifying the main difference of opinion, and what type of difference of opinion it is. A difference of opinion arises when one party's standpoint meets with doubt from the other party. This is an elementary difference of opinion, which is single and nonmixed. If the other party is not only doubtful but adopts an opposing standpoint, then the difference of opinion is mixed. In addition, if there is more than one proposition involved, the difference of opinion is multiple.

1.1   DISAGREEMENT AND ARGUMENTATIVE DISCUSSION

People often disagree with each other. There's nothing special about that. It is unusual, though, for two people to simply accept the fact that their opinions differ and just leave it at that. In many cases, that would be unwise, or even impossible. To resolve the difference of opinion, they need to discuss the matter and try to reach some kind of agreement. If they make use of argumentation as a means to achieve a resolution of a difference, the discussion they are having may be called an *argumentative discussion*. Argumentative discussions are essentially aimed at coming to a reasonable agreement.

In argumentative discussions there is, by definition, an explicit or implicit appeal to reasonableness, but in practice the argumentation can, in all kinds of respects, be lacking in reasonableness. Certain moves can be made in the discussion that are not really helpful to resolving the difference of opinion concerned. Before a well-considered judgment can be given as to the quality of an argumentative discussion, a careful analysis has to be carried out that reveals those aspects of the discourse that are pertinent to making such a judgment concerning its reasonableness. It is the task of the analyst to delve deeply and thoroughly into the various layers of the argumentative text or exchange so that all the relevant elements are taken into account. In the method introduced in this book for analyzing, evaluating, and presenting argumentation, considerable attention is therefore paid to the focal points of argumentative discussion and the ways in which they manifest themselves in the discourse. We start our treatment of the analysis where argumentative discourse also starts in practice, that is, with the difference of opinion that is the source of disagreement.

1.2   EXPLICIT AND IMPLICIT DIFFERENCES OF OPINION

A difference of opinion arises when two parties do not fully agree on a given standpoint. It need not be the case that the second party adopts an opposing standpoint. It is enough that in response to one party's standpoint, the other party has doubts or is not sure:

> Paula: I think schools should spend more time teaching writing skills.
>
> Jack: I don't know, I've never really thought about it.

A *difference of opinion* or disagreement always involves two parties. One party puts forward a standpoint and the other party expresses doubts about it—or, as often happens, goes a step further and rejects the standpoint:

> Paula: I think schools should spend more time teaching writing skills.
>
> Dan: That's ridiculous! More than enough time is spent on that already.

In the preceding example, the difference of opinion is *explicit*: Both the standpoint and the rejection of it are clearly expressed. But this is not always the case. Especially in written texts, the difference of opinion often remains *implicit* because only one party is expressing its views. The other party's skepticism or doubt is anticipated:

> Paula: Schools should spend more time teaching writing skills because students these days have a hard time putting their thoughts on paper. Furthermore, our schools spend ridiculously little time on these skills compared to other countries.

We can be sure that Paula anticipates that her standpoint will not be immediately accepted by everyone because she goes to the trouble of giving arguments in support of it. (Of course it is possible that she is mistaken and that there is, in fact, no difference of opinion between her and her readers.)

1.3   POSITIVE AND NEGATIVE STANDPOINTS

The content of a statement always constitutes a certain *proposition* in which a certain property or quality is ascribed to the persons or things referred to. In a difference of opinion, there are two different positions taken with respect to the proposition a given statement contains. A proposition can be a description of facts or events ("Last year ticket sales at movie theaters declined by 3%"), a prediction ("Knowledge of foreign languages will be an increasingly important requirement in job applications"), a judgment ("Amsterdam is the most beautiful city in Europe"), or advice ("You should brush your teeth with the softest possible toothbrush").

With respect to a proposition, a positive, a negative, or a neutral position can be taken. Dan, Paula, and Alice each take a different position with respect to the proposition that UFOs are a hoax:

> Dan: I think UFOs are a hoax.
> Paula: I don't think UFOs are a hoax.
> Alice: I don't know whether UFOs are a hoax or not.

In this example, Dan has committed himself positively to the proposition that UFOs are a hoax. He has adopted a *positive standpoint* with respect to the proposition. Paula, who believes that UFOs are not a hoax, has committed herself negatively to the proposition; she has adopted a *negative standpoint*. Alice has not committed herself to this proposition in any way because she is not sure about it. For the time being, she is taking a *neutral position*.

In a difference of opinion, there is always at least one person who puts forward a positive or negative standpoint with respect to some proposition, and one person who has doubts or does not commit to any particular standpoint. It may be that the second party not only has doubts but also adopts an opposing standpoint, but this is a more complex form of disagreement that is discussed later.

1.4   STANDPOINTS AND EXPRESSIONS OF DOUBT

Because people can have opinions on any subject whatsoever, the standpoints they adopt can relate to propositions of all kinds. A man may think his wife would look better with a different haircut, that his tennis game will improve if he uses a lighter weight racket, or that methadone should be covered by national health insurance.

Whether a proposition relates to a simple matter or a highly complex matter, it is always possible to adopt a standpoint on it:

> I think Baudelaire is the best French poet.
> Dictators are always right-wing.
> It is bad manners to let an old lady stand when you are seated.
> Behaviorism is an outdated psychological theory.
> The quantum theory is confirmed by the theory of relativity.
> It seems to me her hat was green.
> It's not true that an English mile is the same as two kilometers.
> I don't think we should cancel our property insurance policy.

Propositions on which standpoints are adopted can vary not only in subject matter but also in *scope*. A proposition can apply to everyone or only to certain individuals; it can apply to a whole class or to only part of a class. The *force* of a standpoint taken on a proposition can vary as well. An opinion can be stated with total conviction or, at the other extreme, it can be cautiously expressed as a suggestion. Standpoints can thus vary in degree of force and scope:

> I'm certain that everyone knows fear.
> I suspect that everyone knows fear.

It seems likely that zinc deficiency delays sexual development in some males.

It is doubtful that all words are translatable.

I assume that even intelligent people occasionally have dumb ideas.

You must have added this up wrong.

There's no doubt that everybody needs somebody.

There's no doubt that some people can get along very well by themselves.

It may be that a standpoint addresses more than one proposition at once. Usually, though, these propositions are closely connected to each other. Their connectedness is sometimes made overt by combining them into a single sentence with conjunctions such as *and* and *but:*

It is unacceptable to me for you to go into my room without asking, take books out of my bookshelf, and then lend them to someone else.

It seems to me it is not necessary to take vitamin B complex and vitamin C pills at every meal, but that it's sufficient to take vitamins A and D once a week and vitamin B complex and vitamin C just once in a while.

When someone expresses a positive standpoint, it is sometimes difficult to separate the standpoint from the proposition to which it is related ("Rock concerts are fun"). The proposition and the standpoint taken on it are often combined in a single statement, and the positive nature of the standpoint is often not emphasized, although sometimes it is:

My standpoint is that it really is true that women are more inclined to hysteria than men are.

Like Andrew, I believe that Christianity and pessimism are irreconcilable.

Another complication is that it is often extremely difficult to differentiate between a negative standpoint and an expression of doubt (a neutral position). A cautiously formulated negative standpoint can sound very much like doubt. A statement that on the surface seems to express doubt may, therefore, on closer inspection, actually turn out to function as a negative standpoint. This is quite common because, out of politeness, people usually prefer not to make their disagreement too obvious. There is an inclination to present a negative standpoint as mere skepticism:

> I wonder if that's really such a good idea.

Even though expressions of doubt may seem to be thinly disguised negative standpoints, their consequences are not the same. Adopting a negative standpoint leads to the obligation to defend that negative standpoint if it is called into question, whereas merely expressing doubt does not create any such commitment to defend a standpoint. Therefore, in analyzing argumentation, it is important to determine whether someone is only expressing doubt or may be considered to be adopting a negative standpoint.

1.5   TYPES OF DIFFERENCES OF OPINION

The simplest type of difference of opinion occurs when a standpoint meets with doubt. This is the *elementary form* of differences of opinion. Because a standpoint can be either positive or negative, there are two variants of the elementary form:

  1 Peter: Danish men are romantic.
    Alice: Are they?
  2 Peter: Danish men are not romantic.
    Alice: I'm not so sure about that.

Because the elementary form of differences of opinion involves only one proposition, it is called *single*. In a single difference of opinion, only one standpoint (whether positive or negative) is adopted and then called into doubt by the other party. Such a difference of opinion is said to be *nonmixed* as well: There is only one party who is committed to defending a standpoint. The elementary form of differences of opinion is thus both single and nonmixed.

Besides single nonmixed differences of opinion, there are also mixed differences of opinion and multiple differences of opinion. These can be combined in various ways to form multiple mixed differences of opinion. When analyzed, such complex differences of opinion must first be broken down into a series of elementary differences of opinion. Altogether, four types of differences of opinion can be distinguished: single nonmixed (the elementary form), single mixed, multiple nonmixed, and multiple mixed.

In a *multiple* difference of opinion, the standpoint relates to more than one proposition. A multiple difference of opinion arises when someone brings up two or more issues at the same time, for example, by giving his standpoint on a whole series of matters or by stating an opinion about a complex theory or about a plan with numerous components. Whenever the standpoint involves more than one proposition on which the other party expresses an opinion, the difference of opinion is a multiple one:

Peter: Danish men are neither romantic nor spiritual, but at least you can depend on them.

Alice: I'm not so sure about all that.

In a *mixed* difference of opinion, opposing standpoints are adopted with respect to the same proposition. One party puts forward a positive standpoint and the other party rejects it (i.e., adopts a negative standpoint) or the other way around. This means that instead of simply expressing doubt, the other party responds by adopting an opposing standpoint:

Peter: Danish men are not romantic.

Alice: I don't agree with you.

It is important to be aware that adopting an opposing standpoint always implies doubt (or lack of full agreement) with respect to the other party's standpoint. After all, if there were no doubt, then there would be full agreement with the standpoint, and putting forward the opposite standpoint would then be pointless. Therefore, any complex difference of opinion can be broken down into two or more elementary differences of opinion. The following single mixed difference of opinion can be analyzed as consisting of two elementary differences of opinion:

Peter: You always react way too fast.

Alice: I do not!

The first elementary difference of opinion consists of Peter's positive standpoint with respect to the proposition "Alice always reacts way too fast" together with Alice's doubt about this standpoint. The second elementary difference of opinion consists of Alice's negative standpoint with respect to the proposition "Alice always reacts way too fast" together with Peter's doubt about that standpoint.

1.6   MAIN AND SUBORDINATE DIFFERENCES OF OPINION

During the discussion occasioned by a difference of opinion, new disagreements often surface as the arguments brought forward in defense of a standpoint meet with doubt or rejection. In trying to identify a difference of opinion, it is therefore important to distinguish between the *main* difference of opinion and any *subordinate* differences of opinion that may arise during the discussion about the main disagreement. Look at the following example:

Alice: Excuse me, but I think this soup is spoiled.

Waiter: Madam, that is impossible.

Alice: But look, there's mold floating around in it.

Waiter: That's not mold, those are little pieces of broccoli.

Alice: Well, I've certainly never seen such strange-looking broccoli before.

The main difference of opinion here is single mixed and relates to the proposition "This soup is spoiled." In addition, there is a multiple mixed subordinate difference of opinion relating to the propositions "There's mold floating in the soup" and "There are little pieces of broccoli floating in the soup."

Instead of being stated at the outset, the main difference of opinion often comes to light gradually, so that what the two parties actually disagree on becomes clear only in the course of the discussion. What also often happens is that the same standpoint is repeated in a somewhat different way. It may look like a totally new standpoint, but more often than not, the new version simply does a better job of stating the standpoint than the original version did:

Alice: The French are chauvinistic. I mean, most French people are chauvinistic. I'll tell you why I think so ...

1.7   HOW TO RECOGNIZE STANDPOINTS AND DOUBT

Certain phrases allow the speaker to indicate explicitly that a standpoint is being taken:

My standpoint is that socioeconomic and cultural differences play a large role in the results of intelligence tests.

We are of the opinion that people should be able to smoke in public places.

Additional expressions used to indicate that a standpoint is being taken include:

> *I think that* men and women should leave each other alone as much as possible.
>
> *If you ask me*, there has not been a real diva since Maria Callas.
>
> *I believe* New York is closer to Philadelphia than to Boston.
>
> *My conclusion is that* the economic convergence theory leads to a faulty interpretation of the evolution of the global economy.
>
> *That's why* Nelly Melba is not nearly as famous as the ice cream dessert named after her.
>
> *It simply isn't true that* engaging in sports is necessarily good for your health.
>
> The spinal column *thus* has three different functions.
>
> *Therefore*, the proposal to make all job titles gender-neutral is unacceptable language tyranny.
>
> *I'm convinced that* girls are better students than boys.

In other cases, the wording strongly suggests that a standpoint is being taken but does not provide certainty because (without more contextual information) it leaves room for a different interpretation:

> *The way I see it*, he's only thinking of his own interests.
>
> *In short*, television has an adverse effect on children's behavior.
>
> *In other words*, the ideal of equal pay for equal work is still out of reach.
>
> *In actual fact*, Napoleon thought his brother would be a handy tool.
>
> *I would go so far as to say that* passive sentences are always more difficult to understand than active sentences.
>
> *All things considered*, that's the best route to take.
>
> *What we need to agree on* is that nobody will go off and leak the news to the press.
>
> *It is nonsense to* consider Popper a positivist.
>
> *It's a good idea to* take out travel insurance.

And then there are also cases where the words themselves do not express a standpoint, but where there is a verbal pattern that often occurs when a standpoint is expressed, thus facilitating recognition:

People *shouldn't* want everything all at once.

All archives *ought to be* open to the public.

Pompous language *should be* avoided.

You must never let yourself become entirely dependent on another person.

That measure *is* unfair.

That you can't sleep *is* a sign that something is wrong.

Looking at the context often makes it possible to decide whether a statement can be analyzed as a standpoint or not. Background information may also be helpful.

Doubt may be even more difficult to recognize than a standpoint because it so often remains implicit. The fact that someone finds it necessary to defend a standpoint is, however, a strong indication that they at least anticipate that their standpoint will meet with doubt. It may be that they thought they saw the other person frown. Or perhaps putting themselves in the other person's shoes has led them to expect to meet with doubt.

Even though doubt is often not explicitly stated, there are certain expressions from which doubt can be inferred:

I don't know whether Prince Alexander had much respect for his father.

I'm not entirely sure you remembered to turn off the gas.

I'm not yet convinced that this new policy is in the best interests of children raised by single parents.

Couldn't it be that she shares in the blame as well?

I don't really understand why those two points of view are irreconcilable.

I'll have to think about whether that's a situation where it would be wise to raise interest rates.

FURTHER READING

The theoretical background of our pragma-dialectical approach is explained in F. H. van Eemeren and R. Grootendorst, *Argumentation, Communication, and Fallacies,* Mahwah, NJ: Lawrence Erlbaum Associates, 1992. For a brief overview of other approaches, such as the "Toulmin model," the "new rhetoric," "informal logic and critical thinking," and "formal dialectics," see F. H. van Eemeren, "The state of the art in argumentation theory," in F. H. van Eemeren (Ed.), *Crucial Concepts in Argumentation Theory*, Amsterdam: Amsterdam University Press, 2001, and for a detailed description of these approaches the handbook *Fundamentals of Argumentation Theory* of F. H. van Eemeren, R. Grootendorst, A. F. Snoeck Henkemans, and others, Mahwah, NJ: Lawrence Erlbaum Associates, 1996.

The different types of differences of opinion distinguished here are explained in more detail in chapter 2 of *Argumentation, Communication, and Fallacies*. For an overview of the state of the art in the various approaches to standpoints, views, or points of view, consult P. Houtlosser, "Points of view," in F. H. van Eemeren (Ed.), *Crucial Concepts in Argumentation Theory*, Amsterdam: Sic Sat, 2001. How the presentation of the standpoint may influence the persuasiveness of the argument is discussed in D. J. O'Keefe, "Standpoint explicitness and persuasive effect: A meta-analytic review of the effects of varying conclusion articulation in persuasive messages," *Argumentation and Advocacy*, 1997, vol. 34, no. 1, pp. 1–13.

EXERCISES

1. Do the following passages contain a standpoint? If so, indicate which utterance functions as the standpoint and explain how you can tell that it functions as such.

    a. *Pavarotti to diet and rest*

      Luciano Pavarotti, the Italian tenor, said yesterday that he had been ordered by doctors to go on a supervised diet and not to sing any opera for six months.

    b. *Re "Central Park Shut to Spray for Virus"*

      To the Editor:

      Having recently migrated from New York (where I lived for 17 years) to Florida, I have noted with interest the mosquito problem back home. Mosquitoes used to be a problem down here, though they were more pesky than lethal. Local authorities have all but eliminated the pest by releasing an enormous amount of dragonflies, which devour the pests at an alarming rate.

      Although I'm no expert on the environmental consequences, it seems to be a reasonably efficient, natural, chemical-free solution to a serious problem. I know that the results locally have been at once profound and effective.

    c. A sacked Roman catholic priest will open his own church next month to conduct weddings for divorced and expectant couples and to bless homosexual relationships. Father Pat Buckly intends marrying couples denied the sacrament under Catholic rules. "I believe marriage is for life, but unfortunately people make mistakes and, when people are sincere, they should be allowed a second chance. That's what I'm giving them," he said.

    d. The idea of random tests for cannabis on drivers is positively Hitlerian. Cannabis stays in the system for up to 60 days. You could be in a room where people are smoking marijuana and be banned from driving 48 hours later.

2. Indicate what difference of opinion is at stake in the following texts and to which of the four types of differences of opinion it belongs.

    a. You should always eat something before you go swimming and you should never go swimming in the ocean when it is low tide, because swimming on an empty stomach gives you cramps and when it is low tide you'll get swept out to sea by the current.

b. *Robson:* Research on artificial intelligence ought to be actively stimulated by the U.S. government.

   Briggs: I totally disagree with that.

c. *Baker:* The granting of the so-called "no claims" bonus by car insurance companies not only serves to encourage drivers not to stop after an accident but it also is not to the advantage of motorists who have never had an accident. I shall present detailed arguments in support of these propositions.

d. Your report "Sissy English lessons may hinder boys" struck a chord. For the past two generations English poetry has been in the hands of people—from T.S. Eliot to present Poet Laureate—who seem to have a marked distaste for rhythm, scansion, rhyme and, above all, for subjects likely to interest boys and men. They seem to be introverts occupied with combing their pink fluffy souls, to the exclusion of half their potential readership.

e. Women should not be licensed to box professionally because pre-menstrual syndrome (PMS) makes them unstable. The British boxing board of control refuses to give a license to British woman boxer Jane Couch, the world welterweight champion. "PMS would be more likely to give women an unfair advantage in the boxing ring than make them unfit to don their gloves," said Katharine Dalton, the gynecological endocrinologist credited with naming the syndrome. "It will make them much more aggressive and better boxers."

f. *Ivan Wolffers:* "Societies that believe they can protect themselves by taking a firm line with individuals who are infected with the virus are doing just about the most ill-advised thing imaginable. They isolate people with HIV/AIDS and think that, in so doing, the virus will also be isolated. It is not so easy to isolate a virus. At worst, you treat a number of people in an inhumane manner and they will make sure that no one finds out that they might have the virus."

g. *Letter to the editor:*

   I must disagree with your identification of the mouse in the illustration from *The Tailor of Gloucester* as a dormouse. The mice in the book were modeled on the ordinary house mouse. The dormouse has a shorter, furry tail and rounded ears and is a reddish color.

h. *Letter to the editor:*

Professor Brandon's assertion that no one who has been repeatedly physically or sexually abused ever "loses" the memory runs counter to present professional understanding of traumatic memory. Professor Alan Scheflin and Dr. David Brown, in the U.S. *Journal of Psychiatry and Law* (vol. 24, 2, Summer, 1996) found that amnesia for childhood sexual abuse was "a robust finding across studies using very different samples and methods of assessment."

i. A City, So Lovely, Through Woody Allen's Lens

To the Editor:

As a filmmaker who has tried to record Manhattan at its most beautiful and charming, I would like to stand behind the position taken by some Greenwich Village residents against New York University's plan to put up a 13-story building on West Third Street, destroying two historic structures, including a house where Edgar Allan Poe once lived (letter, July 25).

There is no question that much of Greenwich Village is New York at its loveliest, and the trick over the years in filming around Washington Square has been to show the world the magic of the great-looking preserved areas while framing out the construction done by N.Y.U.

No one is questioning the need for the university's law school to expand, but surely it can be worked out in a way that does not destroy yet another piece of this fast-vanishing area.

It is hard for me to believe that a great institution like N.Y.U., which had the foresight and good taste to expel me many years ago, would be insensitive to this situation.

WOODY ALLEN

SPECIAL ASSIGNMENT 1

a. Make a review of Texts 1 and 2 in which you:
1. Represent the authors' positions and their main lines of defense.
2. Comment on the quality of the individual arguments.
3. Give your overall judgement of the arguments. Which of the authors has the strongest argument?
b. The review should be approximately 4 pages (double spaced). Make two copies: Submit one copy to the instructor at the next class meeting and one to another student.
c. Before the following class meeting, the students should evaluate each other's reviews and submit their evaluation to the author of the review and to the instructor. In the evaluation report, attention should be paid to the following points:
1. Have the authors' positions and arguments been correctly represented?
2. Does the reader get a clear overview of the organization of the authors' arguments?
3. Does the criticism on individual arguments seem justified? Is it sufficiently supported?
4. Is the overall judgment based on a careful weighing up of the judgments of the individual arguments?
d. The instructor will make some general comments on the reviews and will discuss some problems with the help of a sample of the type of errors encountered in the students' texts.

Text 1

MIDDLE OF THE ROAD
Laurence Deverall

This week's column was what I had prepared for last time but the Add/Drop fracas intervened and provided a bit of diversion. By the cartoons and other responses it engendered it must have put some people under conviction. I have always
5 found that the truth cuts like a knife and stings like salt in an open wound, but in the end acts as a catharsis and cleanses the soul. Thus I intend to keep on doing it. This week I will undoubtedly get more people mad at me.

For the past few years I have noticed several things about a
10 university education: not only does it get progressively more expensive but some of that expense is hard to justify. Books are one such item. Why is it that some textbooks are much more expensive on campus than off it? Now I realize that smaller quantity printings of books call for higher retail prices be-
15 cause the cost of production is higher per book. But when I see the same text book, *The Oxford Illustrated History of Christianity*, which I purchased for $20 (Can) as a bonus book from my book club, offered for sale in the University Bookstore for $55 plus GST, I have to ask why the over 100% increase? Surely
20 bulk purchases should result in even lower prices.

Another question I would like to see answered is why some professors change text books every time they offer the same course? Often some very expensive books that students have HAD to buy are rendered valueless after one semester. Stu-
25 dents have few other options than to drop the thing in the trash can if it is no part of their major. Many books at the IVCF second-hand book sale this year fell into this category. For students who rely on the resale of books to offset the cost of the next semester's books, this can be a real hardship.

30 One reason that could be offered for this situation is that the sum total of knowledge is doubling every few months and so new text books are needed. But surely not every discipline is

changing so fast that the texts are out of date in four months!
No, there must be other reasons for the switching.

I have discovered, I think, a significant chain of events that 35
may help explain why students are suckered into forking out
excessive cash for books. First, in order to get research funding
from the government (which helps to pay profs' salaries) the
University has to have the profs doing research. One of my instructors told me that only 20% of his time was spent on class 40
related activities, the remainder was spent on research, book
writing and committee meetings.

Secondly, profs have to prove they are doing research by
publishing their findings. If they do not, they will not get increases in salary and, in fact, may lose their jobs. This hap- 45
pened to one of my profs—he spent too much time helping his
students and was given the Royal Order of the Boot.

Thirdly, it costs money to publish books, particularly in
small quantities in less popular disciplines. Someone has to
pay for these books and, you guessed it, it's the students. I 50
would hate to suggest that our illustrious teachers go to their
annual conferences to look at their colleagues' new books offered for sale at the publisher's book fairs (which, quite coinci-
dentally, are held in conjunction with these events) and agree
to make those new books required texts for their next classes. 55
The possibility of such collusion certainly exists. Thus there is
a potential conflict of interest which in the end costs students
extra money to grease the wheels of the system.

Is it possible that in reality universities don't exist for the
benefit of students but function only to provide places in 60
which academics and administrators can pursue their careers?
Could it be that we students are only an unwanted but necessary adjunct to a university's activities? I think we need to let
the establishment know that we are not just an intrusion into
their working day but the very reason for their existence. If we 65
do this, who knows, we might just end up a little better off in
pocket for our labors.

Text 2

DEVERALL'S "DRIVEL" DECONSTRUCTED
David Ingham (Department of English)

Since he finished a degree at the U of L., Laurence Deverall should certainly know better than to write the unresearched, prof-bashing drivel which appeared in his last column ("Middle of the Road," 26 Sept), and while it should be obvious that
5   his allegations shouldn't be taken seriously, it's just possible that some of your readers might mistakenly think there is something to them.

First of all, the suggestion that there is a conspiracy among faculty to bilk impoverished students of their much needed
10   money by forcing them to buy inferior, overpriced texts written by faculty colleagues is as ludicrous as it is repugnant. But Mr. Deverall's "logic" is skewed at every step. He notes that faculty are expected to do research, and show evidence of that by publishing, but either suppresses or didn't bother
15   to find out the facts that 1) the overwhelming majority of what we publish is *articles* (in scholarly journals) and not books, and 2) of those academic books which do get published, the vast majority are not suitable for use as undergraduate texts. They're much more likely to be of interest
20   only to specialists in the field, and libraries. (By the way, they aren't like novels—we don't get royalties or anything like that.) And when we do go to "book fairs" at the conference of Learned Societies (the conference of conferences), where we see our colleagues' new books, our text orders have already
25   been in for a month. Moreover, the titles at these "book fairs" are unlikely to be suitable as texts anyway: *We buy them for ourselves.* [sic] (Logical, when you think about it—the very latest, most advanced and specialized research is rather often beyond what we can expect of the average undergradu-
30   ate.) In actuality, the way we find out about potential new texts is through the publisher's reps who regularly come around to our office flogging their wares.

I'll tell you why we do change texts, however. Often it's because there's a new edition out, and since the old edition goes
out of print—which I agree it sometimes does with suspicious 35
frequency—we couldn't keep using it if we wanted to (I've
tried). Or we come across a better text; you do want us to use
the best texts we can, don't you, as long as they're comparable
in price (or cheaper). Sometimes we find a text just as good (or
nearly so), but substantially cheaper, surely you'd prefer for 40
us to switch in those cases. And once in a while we switch just
for the sake of variety. Would you want to take a course from
someone who's been giving exactly the same lectures on exactly the same books for twenty years? We do care about our
students, and definitely sympathize with them over high text 45
prices (I support a student, so I do know about it, too).

So put up or shut up, Mr. Deverall. Name names—supply
evidence. I want to know just which faculty members have deleted texts and changed to ones which are a) inferior, b) more
expensive, and c) written by friends. If you can't, then an apol- 50
ogy and a retraction is in order. When you say, "I would hate to
suggest ... " and then go on to do exactly that, you move only
from the realm of legally actionable slander to that of slimy in-
sinuation.

In addition, there are a few other problems with your col- 55
umn. For one thing, don't blame the bookstore for high prices.
They have no choice but to pay whatever the publisher
charges, and their mark-up is designed specifically to break
even (in fact, they lose money on books, and make it up on
clothing). Did it ever occur to you that maybe, just maybe, the 60
reason you got your book so cheaply from the bookclub was
not because the bookstore is trying to rip you off, but because
your wealthy book club was giving you a discount???

You also imply that most faculty devote too little time to
teaching, and that those who do care about their students risk 65
dismissal. Balderdash. Faculty here are required to meet minimum standards in three areas, teaching, research, and service.
To spend time on only one of these three to the exclusion of the
other two is to refuse to comply with the conditions of employment. And when you quote one of your instructors as claiming 70
to spend only "20% of his time on class related activities," you
conveniently neglect to say 20% of *what*. Twenty percent of 100
hours a week? Remember, 20% of 40 hours is only eight, which

75 is a bit difficult to believe if he's spending nine hours a week in the classroom. (In case anyone's interested, judging by my own discipline—English—your instructors likely spend an average of between 10 and 20 hours per week per course, counting teaching, preparation, marking, seeing students and so on.)

80   Finally, I am shocked and appalled at your apparent assumption that students who purchase texts which are "not part of their major" will automatically either sell them, or if they can't be sold, "drop the[m] in the trash can." I hope and pray that at least a few students here occasionally take courses

85 outside their majors just because they're interested, and might even believe that at least some of the text books they bought are valuable in and of *themselves*, not just at the cash register. Believe it or not, some of us were actually brought up to *respect* books, and to care about other things than money. So if a text is

90 of no use to you, and you can't sell it, for God's sake don't just "drop the thing in the trash can," *donate it to the library.* Perhaps someone else can find value in it.

    In conclusion, the professors at this University are here primarily because of their students—it's a pretty stupid career

95 choice for anyone who's not. And unless you produce some evidence to support your defamatory allegations, it certainly looks as if we care a good deal more about our students, Mr. Deverall, than you do about the truth.

2

Argumentation and Discussion

A critical discussion is an ideal of argumentative discourse aimed at resolving a difference of opinion by determining whether the standpoints at issue ought to be accepted or not. A critical discussion proceeds through four stages: the confrontation, opening, argumentation, and concluding stages. In practice, argumentative discourse corresponds only partly with this ideal model and it may also be the case that only one of the parties expresses its view, so that the discussion remains implicit. An analysis of argumentative discourse must examine to what extent the discourse can be reconstructed as a critical discussion.

2.1 RESOLVING A DIFFERENCE OF OPINION

A difference of opinion is said to be resolved as soon as one of the two parties revise their original position. If the difference of opinion is an elementary one, resolution is reached when the doubting party abandons his or her doubts, or when the other party retreats from his or her standpoint:

> At first I wasn't sure whether I agreed with you, but I have to admit you are right.
>
> Now that I've heard all of your reservations, I've come to think my standpoint isn't so strong after all.

The end of active disagreement does not necessarily mean that the difference of opinion has truly been resolved. It is important to distinguish between *resolving* a difference of opinion and merely *settling* it. Settling a disagreement means that it is simply set aside. This can be achieved in an uncivilized manner by intimidating or forcing the other party into submission. A civilized, but arbitrary, way of settling a disagreement is to lay the matter before a third party who serves as judge and decides who is right. Another civilized way of settling a disagreement is to decide the winner by drawing lots. Still another way is to put the matter to a vote and let the majority decide:

> During the health care debate, the Italian Prime Minister got his way by forcing the issue to a vote, which the socialist party lost. Clearly, however, not all of the socialist members of the Cabinet are convinced of the desirability of the new policy measures.

In such cases, the difference of opinion has not really been resolved. True resolution is reached only if both parties come to hold the same position on the grounds of rational argumentation. Either both parties adopt the same standpoint (positive or negative) or else both parties begin to question the standpoint.

2.2   A MODEL OF A CRITICAL DISCUSSION

To be able to deal with a difference of opinion in a rational way, there needs to be an *argumentative discussion*. This is a discussion in which argumentation is used to try to determine to what extent a given standpoint is defensible. The purpose of an argumentative discussion is different from that of an *informative discussion*, which serves primarily to convey information.

In real-life discussions, informative and argumentative elements are often combined. Once the participants realize that their viewpoints differ, it is usually not long before they decide to attempt to find out which view is the most tenable, and this, in turn, requires a thorough knowledge of each other's viewpoints. When the discussion is not simply aimed at informing someone about something, it is best to view it as an argumentative discussion.

Ideally, an argumentative discussion is a *critical discussion* aimed at resolving a difference of opinion. A critical discussion takes place between a party who defends a certain (positive or negative) standpoint, the *protagonist*, and a party who challenges this standpoint, the *antagonist*. Only when an antagonist counters the standpoint of the protagonist with an opposing standpoint is this antagonist also the protagonist of a standpoint. During the discussion, protagonists try to convince antagonists of the acceptability of their standpoints, while the antagonists keep raising doubts or objections.

A critical discussion aimed at resolving a difference of opinion proceeds through four stages, which are distinguished analytically in the following model:

1. In the *confrontation stage* the parties establish that they have a difference of opinion. In a nonmixed difference of opinion, this simply means that one party's standpoint is not immediately accepted by the other party, but is met with doubt or criticism. In a mixed difference of opinion, the other party advances the opposite standpoint.
2. In the *opening stage* the parties decide to try to resolve the difference of opinion. They assign the roles of protagonist and antagonist (in a mixed difference, there are two protagonists and two antagonists). They also agree on the rules for the discussion and on the starting points.
3. In the *argumentation stage* the protagonist defends his or her standpoint against the sometimes persistent criticism of the antagonist by putting forward arguments to counter the antagonist's objections or to remove the antagonist's doubts.
4. In the *concluding stage* the parties assess the extent to which the difference of opinion has been resolved and in whose favor. If the protagonist withdraws the standpoint, the difference of opinion is resolved in favor of the antagonist; if the antagonist abandons his or her doubts, it is resolved in favor of the protagonist.

2.3   THE IDEAL MODEL AND ARGUMENTATIVE PRACTICE

Of course an ideal model does not describe reality. And yet, real-life argumentative discussions do sometimes approach the model. In an article in a Dutch sports magazine, the author's contribution to the discussion comes very close to following the model:

> *The Light Athletic Association leadership recently met to discuss the future of athletics. This is undoubtedly a praiseworthy effort. Dick Loman gave an enthusiastic report of this meeting and invited anyone not present to join in the discussion. I am answering his call by expressing my opinion in this article.*
>
> Part of the discussion concerns whether or not to further centralize the training of athletes. And this is the point I would like to speak to.
>
> For years, centralized training has bothered me ... Not because of ... but primarily because ...
>
> And so, I repeat: do away with centralized training.

In the italicized introduction, the author announces her status as protagonist. Apart from this announcement, there is no reference to the opening stage. The author proceeds with the confrontation by putting forward the standpoint that centralized training should be done away with. The argumentation stage is complete. (To save space it has not been repeated here.) The concluding stage is also explicit, even though the author, in giving the conclusion, of course speaks only for herself.

It is quite common for little time to be spent on the *opening* of a discussion. Discussion rules and other starting points are often taken for granted and do not require explicit mention. This is not entirely correct, however. It is precisely the lack of "proper procedure" in a discussion—the lack of explicit rules—that causes many discussions to run into difficulty.

The *conclusion* of a discussion is more often explicit, though seldom as explicitly expressed as in the following newspaper column:

> A discussion about the relationship between parliament and public opinion could be fascinating, but not with Polly Toynbee. I hereby declare that I have won the discussion and will now go on to more important matters.

Polly Toynbee, in her reply, seems to have no expectation that the discussion can be concluded with agreement on both sides:

> Let me be frank: if I have a debate with someone, I never have the illusion that my opponent will say at the end: "Polly Toynbee, you are right; I have made a mistake; from now on I shall defend your standpoint."

This is taking things too far. And yet, it is highly desirable that both parties should reach agreement on the outcome of the discussion. Fortunately, many discussions do end in agreement on the outcome, or at least come close to it. Note that even in the case of discussions decided by voting, it is desirable that both parties reach agreement on the outcome:

> It was gratifying that the membership of the party, after thorough consideration, decided unanimously in favor of proposition 102.

Most argumentative discussions, then, depart considerably from the model. The parties often do not go through all four of the discussion stages or not in the same order. Sometimes one party declares that the difference of opinion has been decided in its favor before the argumentation stage has even been completed. Sometimes, in the course of the discussion, the parties realize they have failed to clearly identify what exactly they disagree on, so that it becomes necessary to go back to the confrontation stage. Elements of the different stages may be missing that are indispensable for the resolution of the difference of opinion. The discussion may also contain a great many elements (e.g., expressions of courtesy, jokes, and anecdotes) that, without directly contributing to the resolution, help to make the discussion go more smoothly.

Such discrepancies between theory and practice do not diminish the usefulness of the model. By definition, an ideal differs from reality. The idealized model has an important critical function: It can be a tool for identifying where a real-life argumentative discussion goes wrong. It makes it possible to identify what necessary elements are missing or inadequately represented. For example, comparison with the model makes it possible to say that, in one instance, the discussion fails because the difference of opinion has not been clearly identified, whereas in another instance it fails because roles have not been properly assigned or because discussion rules have not been agreed on.

The model of a critical discussion is more than a tool for evaluating whether the discussion has proceeded correctly. It is also an instrument for analyzing a discussion (whether simple or complex) in a constructive manner. In this regard it has a heuristic function: Elements that are only implicitly present in the discussion can more easily be identified, and the various elements of the discussion can be analyzed in a way that clarifies their role in the resolution process.

2.4   ARGUMENTATION IN AN IMPLICIT CRITICAL DISCUSSION

Most people regard the argumentation stage as the "real" discussion. It does in fact largely determine the outcome. Taken together, the arguments used by the protagonist in the argumentation stage to make a case are what constitute a discursive text. In other words, a discursive text, or case, is the sum total of all argumentation brought forward to defend a standpoint.

In a nonmixed difference of opinion, there is always just one party who presents a case, however simple or complex this argument may be. The antagonist simply asks questions and does not adopt a standpoint. In a mixed difference of opinion, each party has a standpoint that requires defending; therefore, each party presents a case.

> Paula: It seems to me it's to my advantage that I have never done anything like this before.
>
> Jack: That's not an advantage if you ask me.
>
> Paula: Why not?
>
> Jack: You first explain why you think it's an advantage, and then I'll tell you why I think it's not.
>
> Paula: Well, as far as I'm concerned, it's pretty simple: the fact that I have no experience means that I approach it with no preconceived notions. And for a screen test that's important.
>
> Jack: It's not at all an advantage to do a screen test with no experience, because you have no idea what to do to present yourself in the most favorable light. And that's really tricky.

During the latter part of this discussion, Paula and Jack each present a case for their standpoint. Here their arguments are part of an explicit discussion, but more often than not arguments are part of an *implicit discussion*. An implicit discussion is one in which only one of the parties participates.

Even if the other party does not explicitly participate, however, this party's point of view is still taken into account. This may, for instance, become apparent when the protagonist explicitly refers to the potential objections of a real or imagined antagonist:

> There's no other country in the world where women are as well integrated into the army as in Norway—and don't go bringing up the case of Israel, because in Israel women don't

fight in the front lines. Have you ever seen women soldiers in one of those intifadah photos?

A practical complication is that argumentation sometimes takes the form of a monologue and it is hard to recognize any of the elements of a discussion. Even so, a monologue defending a standpoint should be viewed as a one-way dialogue. Such monologues are so common that people don't even realize that argumentative discourse always presumes a discussion or dialogue situation, even though it may be implicit. Argumentation always has the aim of convincing potential critics, whether or not they are actually present.

If the discussion remains implicit, parties putting forward their case as a rule need to do more than just present their argumentation. They need to incorporate the other stages of the discussion process in their case as well, and perhaps point out potential doubts and known objections. At the outset they need to establish that a difference of opinion exists or threatens to arise (*confrontation stage*). Next, they have to make it clear that they are prepared to resolve the difference by following certain rules for argumentative discussions; they may briefly mention these rules and any starting points (*opening stage*). Then of course they present their own argumentation, perhaps referring to the views of an opposing party (*argumentation stage*). Finally, they need to assess to what extent the difference of opinion has been resolved by their argumentation (*concluding stage*). This is more or less what happens in the following case:

> A lot of people have been saying recently that penalties for criminals should be stiffer. I don't agree with this and I will explain why. First I will review all the arguments I've heard in favor of stiffer penalties and show why they are unsound.
> [...]
> I believe I have conclusively shown that stiffer penalties for criminals don't make any sense. This is a matter on which reasonable people need no longer disagree.

There are instances in which the antagonist at whom the case is directed is not specified; it may be entirely unclear who the potential antagonist might be. But when argumentation is analyzed, we proceed from the assumption that it is an attempt by the speaker to convince someone who does not yet agree with the speaker's standpoint. After all, if everyone already agreed, there would be no reason to go to the trouble to argue the case.

FURTHER READING

In theories of critical discussion, informal as well as formal models have been developed. The informal model which constitutes the basis for this book can be found in F. H. van Eemeren and R. Grootendorst, *Speech Acts in Argumentative Discussions*, Dordrecht/Berlin: Foris/Walter de Gruyter, 1984, and *Argumentation, Communication, and Fallacies: A Pragma-Dialectical Perspective*, Hillsdale, NJ: Lawrence Erlbaum Associates, 1992. Formal models of argumentative discussions aimed at resolving a dispute are studied in "dialogue logic." See, for instance, E. M. Barth and E. C. W. Krabbe, *From Axiom to Dialogue: A Philosophical Study of Logics and Argumentation*, Berlin: Walter de Gruyter, 1982, and D. N. Walton and E. C. W. Krabbe, *Commitment in Dialogue*, Albany, NY: State University of New York Press, 1995. In "Disputation by design," *Argumentation*, 1998, vol. 12, no. 2, pp. 183–198, S. Jackson discusses the use of models of argumentative discussions for localizing problems in discussions on the World Wide Web.

EXERCISES

1. Each of the following passages is part of an argumentative discussion. Indicate to which discussion stage or stages it belongs.
   a. I think it would be very interesting to see whether I can convince you of the opposite point of view. But you should first let me finish my argument before you respond. And we should not resort to any kind of cheap trick such as constantly quoting important people who share our views.
   b. In the end I have to admit that Johnson's last argument is convincing enough to make me doubt whether the solution I proposed is really so desirable.
   c. *Prison director:* "It is just fashionable nonsense to think that it doesn't make any difference whether you work in a prison or in a car factory. It is this strange tension in a prison that appeals to me. In prison, no two days are alike. Say what you like about the people I'm dealing with, but they are never dull or predictable."
   d. As a practicing psychotherapist, I found much to disagree with in your article "Child abuse memories." Your claims about the advantages of hypnosis are wrong. I have seen the process of false memory produced by hypnosis and suggestion. I would not rely on any "memory recovery technique." To encourage someone to believe they were abused is unlikely to make their lives better. It might even be harmful. The psychotherapist or psychiatrist is not an investigator or detective. The psychiatrist is in no position to decide who is telling the truth. This is the opinion of many professional psychotherapists and you should know better.
   e. Robert Buderi's thesis is that the invention and development of radar in the Second World War changed the post-war world. Specifically, Dr. Buderi asserts that many of the devices that govern lives today—computers, microwaves, lasers, rockets, commercial and military activities in space—are a direct result of the concentration of many scientists on radar during the war. The proposition is interesting, but not supported by the miscellaneous collection of chapters in this book, with their heavy bias towards American scientists and technology. In the following I will show why.
   f. *Letter to the editor:*
      Speak for yourself, Kate Figes, about how motherhood

turns intelligent women into fearful, watchful, exhausted, children's-TV-watching mommy blobs. I was determined to avoid this stuff—and did.

When my children were younger, I kept all my childless friends, had some evenings out, read books, took fitness classes, held a demanding job and still had time to spend with the tots. And if you have a reasonable partner, there's no reason that each of you can't go away on your own for a few days from time to time. Sure, having children is a big job, but this kind of wallowing in earth-mother self-indulgence makes it even harder for mothers to take full part in the workforce and society; such an article makes childless women and most men regard women as self-absorbed, helpless homebodies who aren't fit for the mainstream.

2. a. Which parts of the contributions of Andy, Brian and Colin can be regarded as part of (1) the confrontation stage, (2) the opening stage, (3) the argumentation stage, and (4) the concluding stage?

   b. Which parts of the discussion are not relevant to the resolution of the dispute?

   A   *Andy:*   Now that I've got you for a moment—have you got round to thinking about your birthday yet? Are you having people over or not?

   B   *Brian:*   I was thinking of having a party, actually. Not a bad idea it seems to me. What do you think? Why don't we get straight down to it and work out who I'm going to invite—I mean, am I going to ask Christine or not?

   C   *Andy:*   Christine? Of course you'll ask her. You must!

   D   *Brian:*   Actually, I don't think I ought to.

   (Enter Colin. He joins Andy and Brian.)

   E   *Colin:*   What's new?

   F   *Brian:*   What do you mean new? Hey, have some coffee.

   G   *Andy:*   Hi, Colin. Dropped in at the right moment again, didn't you?

   H   *Colin:*   This coffee is much too strong again. What were you talking about?

   I   *Brian:*   Whether I ought to ask Christine to my party.

   J   *Colin:*   Course you should.

   K   *Andy:*   You keep out of this Colin. Let Brian decide that for himself in peace. I'd just like to know, Brian, exactly why you object to Christine coming.

L   *Colin:*   She can come as far as I'm concerned!

M   *Andy:*   I'm sure your girlfriend would like to hear that. But I just happen to be talking to Brian. If you don't mind: what's the objection of her coming? It's your birthday, so you decide.

N   *Brian:*   But you're the one who's so interested in inviting her. *I* think *you* should start by telling us why it's so important that she should come.

O   *Andy:*   I've told you, it's your birthday, so it's up to *you* to say why she isn't welcome.

P   *Brian:*   That's all very well, but I have the strong impression that *you've* some reason of your own. So you've got to say why, too.

Q   *Colin:*   Are you two managing to work things out? Just invite her, will you? Stop going on about it all the time.

R   *Andy:*   Do you want it to be another one of those awful drags? ... Christine is the nicest woman I've met in a long time.

S   *Brian:*   And you wanted me to stay away, did you? I can't ask Christine: Michael would come too, the creep!

T   *Andy:*   Okay then: exit Christine.

U   *Colin:*   Figured it out, have we?

V   *Andy:*   Just give me a beer.

W   *Brian:*   Okay, so what are we doing? Asking her?

X   *Andy:*   No, no I said you were right, didn't I? Have it your own way. Don't bother.

3. The adult education center in London offers courses in "conversation and discussion techniques." In one of these courses, a role play was performed that takes place in the board room of Harrods department store. The following is an excerpt from this role play.

  a. Which parts of the contributions to the discussion by the chairman and by Mrs. Hans can be assigned to (1) the confrontation stage, (2) the opening stage, (3) the argumentation stage, and (4) the concluding stage?

  b. Explain why the contributions to the discussion by Mrs. Hans in F and S are not part of a critical discussion aimed at resolving a disagreement.

  c. Has the main dispute in this discussion been resolved or merely settled?

A   *Chairman:*   If everyone is present then I would like to welcome everyone to the meeting. I believe the problem is clear. We have a shortage of personnel and new workers cannot be found. We have received an offer from an organization for job placement of discharged prisoners that would make ex-prisoners available to us as employees. Mrs. Foster is present as an expert to tell us more about this. I would then like to open up the matter for discussion. I would also like to mention that, if at all possible, this meeting ought to be concluded within twenty minutes.

(The explanation by Mrs. Foster follows.)

B   *Chairman:*   If all of this is clear, then I would like to hear the opinion of those involved.

C   *Mrs. Hans:*   Well, in my view it is sheer madness to employ a bunch of discharged prisoners, and that twenty per cent of my staff members are to be replaced by criminals. I have to put them next to a cash register and they cannot be trusted, because, in my view, normal people do not end up in prison; so I think it's an absurd idea to employ discharged prisoners at Harrods. This company has a good name and you just cannot put these people there!

D   *Mr. Jones:*   Well, I would very much like to know who exactly is to come. If these are people who have committed minor offenses, then that's all right. I would rather have someone who has committed a traffic offense than someone who has stolen something. After all, once a thief, always a thief. That's my opinion!

E   *Mrs. Foster:*   Now, I understand that Mrs. Hans believes the entire situation to be rather absurd. That's a shame. Statistics show that others— including the management of Woolworth's —are really quite satisfied with the employment of discharged prisoners. In terms of percentage, there is no risk whatsoever. The percentage of repeat offenders is the same as the percentage of the population that steals for the first time.

F   *Mrs. Hans:*   Well, if that's the case, then I can't really say anything more against it. But I still can't agree to it.

G *Mr. Bowers:*   I think that they ought to be put to work in the administrative department; a stolen paper-clip isn't so bad.

H   *Mr. Jones:*   Yes, but the administrative department contains personal details of staff members. It is, after all, not so very wise to let thieves have access to that information.

I   *Mr. Bowers:*   Well, that's true.

J   *Mrs. Hans:*   It's simply insane. A bunch of thieves in the sales department.

K   *Mr. Jones:*   But after all, that's not to say they will all start stealing again, is it?

L   *Mrs. Hans:*   Well, once a thief, always a thief, that's what you just said yourself!

M   *Mr. Jones:*   You're probably right. Are there any financial guarantees?

N *Mrs. Foster:*   Yes, indeed there are. Any damage that might be caused by these discharged prisoners will be compensated for.

O   *Mr. Jones:*   Well, in that case, I can't see any real objections any more. We ought to give these people a chance.

P *Mr. Bowers:*   We are not a social institution, we are a commercial company!

Q *Mrs. Hans:*   Exactly! No criminals in my department!

R   *Mr. Jones:*   Well, well, what arguments do you have for the proposition that you can still regard them as criminals?

S   *Mrs. Hans:*   Well, I don't know. They simply are, that's all.

T   *Chairman:*   Well, it seems to me it's time to make a decision. Are there still people who have insurmountable objections to the employment of discharged prisoners in our company?

U *Mrs. Hans:*   Yes, me!

V   *Chairman:*   Good. No one else? Then I think we are decided. Only one vote against. Going on the statistics, we conclude that it is a responsible decision to employ these people in the company. Mrs. Foster, thank you for your information. Thanks to everyone for taking part in this discussion, and have a safe trip home.

3
Standpoints and Argumentation

ESSENTIALS

*A*lthough argumentation in defense of a standpoint is usually not explicitly presented as such, the discourse often contains indicators of argumentation. Some are part of a "progressive" presentation, in which the standpoint being defended follows the argumentation; others are part of a "retrogressive" presentation, in which the standpoint precedes the argumentation. Problems of interpretation are more likely to arise in an unclear context than in a well-defined context. When they arise, the analyst must rely on background information or, when such information is not available, choose the interpretation that is maximally argumentative.

3.1 IDENTIFYING THE STANDPOINT

In order to determine how a difference of opinion has been resolved, one must first identify what arguments the speaker or writer has advanced in defense of his or her standpoint. There are several different types of clues in the verbal presentation that can help with the identification of arguments.

The purpose of argumentation is always to defend a standpoint. If the standpoint is a positive one, defending it consists of *justifying* the proposition to which the standpoint refers:

> It's true that TV makes life more fun, because since we've had television, we don't play card games any more.

If the argumentation is used to defend a negative standpoint, then it is intended to *refute* the proposition:

> It's not true that TV makes life more fun, because since we've had television, we don't play card games any more.

Argumentation is thus always an attempt either to justify or to refute something. But how does one determine that such an attempt is being made? How can argumentation be recognized? What are the clues?

The utterances that together form the argumentation are always related to a certain standpoint. Identifying this standpoint is usually the first step toward identifying the argumentation. If the standpoint is presented with great conviction, one can expect the defense of it to follow very shortly:

> I'm telling you *that plan is totally crazy*. As far as I know, none of the necessary preparation has been done and you're the last person who could ever accomplish it.

A standpoint is seldom an utterance whose acceptability is clearly evident. This explains why an unusual or controversial statement or other utterance that is not in line with expectations is readily taken to be a standpoint. The question then arises what arguments are put forward in defense of this standpoint. Usually these arguments are quick to appear:

> You should never believe what your own partner says. A partner always looks at you through rose-colored glasses.

In analyzing argumentative discourse, the verbal presentation should ideally carry the most weight. One needs to watch out for indicators of standpoints such as *in my opinion* and *I think that* and for other expressions that suggest a standpoint, such as *I conclude by saying that* ... and *I hope I have shown that* ... Once it has been determined what the standpoint is, it is easier to figure out which utterances form the argumentation for this standpoint.

3.2   INDICATORS OF ARGUMENTATION

Sometimes speakers announce that the utterances they are about to produce have an argumentative function ("My arguments for this are ..."). Sometimes argumentation is labeled as such by a comment at the end ("I have concluded my defense"). Such explicit announcements, however, are the exception rather than the rule.

In everyday communication, the intended function of utterances is not normally indicated explicitly. Only when absolutely necessary to avoid misunderstanding, for legal or formal reasons or for emphasis, is the function of an utterance explicitly characterized:

> I hereby *declare* this court in session.
>
> We strongly *advise* you to leave the university and put your talents to use in another way.
>
> It will never happen again. And that's a *promise*.

Speakers or writers who want to make clear that what follows is argumentation do not necessarily need to resort to explicit announcements; they can also use indicators of argumentation. Good examples of these are *therefore, thus, so, consequently, of course, because, since, given that.* The following horoscope contains several such indicators:

> Aries—21 March through 20 April—Usually you are neither organized nor thorough. Making plans is foreign to your nature, and the very idea of following through on details makes you ill. *Therefore* you will never become a scientist and certainly never win the Nobel prize.
>
> Leo—21 July through 20 August—In the course of the coming week you will again find yourself in a situation where your critical thinking is not appreciated. Especially when you use that sharp tongue of yours to express it. *So* keep this part of your anatomy under control, *for*, as the Bible says, "The tongue is a great evil, full of deadly poison."

As a rule, indicators of argumentation also serve as indicators of standpoints. So, in the search for the standpoint, it comes in handy when an indicator of argumentation is present. Sometimes indicators refer to a standpoint that was stated earlier: for example, *because* and *since*. This order of presentation is *retrogressive*, that is, the standpoint is given before the argument:

Children must learn not to instantly satisfy every urge they feel *because* otherwise they would sit in front of the TV eating chips all day long.

Other indicators of argumentation signal that a standpoint will follow, for example in the conclusion. Such indicators include *thus, for that reason,* and *therefore.* This is *progressive* presentation:

Children who watch television as much as they want to don't get their homework done. *Therefore,* parents should limit their children's access to television.

Other words and expressions are less obvious indicators of argumentation: *on one hand ... on the other hand, this is evidence of, on the grounds of, firstly ... secondly, because of, ought to, should, all in all, in short.* When these indicators are used, they often signal argumentation:

In view of the fact that he was the one who canceled the appointment, he *ought* to be the one to arrange a new appointment.

Some expressions, such as *all in all,* point to argumentation because they are indicators of a standpoint while making at the same time clear that argumentation has been provided for this standpoint. But all these expressions may also be used in situations that are not argumentative. Even a word like *so,* though it often indicates an argument, does not always indicate an argument because it is also used as a filler:

So then I asked her when she was going to leave, and she got mad, *so* she slammed the door in my face, *so* that's the last I've seen of her.

3.3   CLUES IN THE CONTEXT

In practice, there is often no indicator of argumentation and it is sometimes not immediately obvious whether the presentation is progressive or retrogressive:

Carla doesn't ever want to see Bob again. She won't call him.

Two argumentative interpretations of this discourse fragment are possible:

1 (*retrogressive presentation*) Carla doesn't ever want to see Bob again, *because* she won't call him.

2 (*progressive presentation*) Carla doesn't ever want to see Bob again, *so* she won't call him.

"Carla doesn't ever want to see Bob again" could be the standpoint here (interpretation 1), or it could be "Carla won't call Bob" (interpretation 2). In the former case the argument is "she won't call him;" in the latter case it is "she doesn't ever want to see him again." In the original discourse fragment, there is no way to tell from the wording which of the interpretations is the correct one. If the utterance were spoken, the speaker's intonation might provide a clue.

Usually, implicit standpoints and argumentation occur in a *context* that helps to clarify their function. For example, someone may have just remarked that Carla will probably be getting together with Bob soon. Or there may have been discussion about whether Carla will be calling Bob or not. In a well-defined context like that it is not difficult to decide on the correct interpretation. Problems of interpretation usually arise in a context that is not well defined, that is, where there are no clues.

A well-defined context may consist of utterances following or preceding the utterance whose function is unclear. Additional information from other sources, such as "Bob hasn't heard from her in weeks" makes it clear that "Carla doesn't ever want to see Bob again" is the standpoint and not "Carla won't call Bob." It can be assumed that the speaker considers "Carla won't call Bob" to be an established fact and not a standpoint that requires defending; otherwise, that additional remark would be difficult to explain.

A reference to the difference of opinion that needs resolving or of the standpoint to which the argumentation is related can also help provide a well-defined context that makes interpretation easier. Another way the context can signal that something is an argument is when the presumed argument is directly preceded or followed by a claim that is so clearly unacceptable that it almost has to be a standpoint that needs defending. In the following example, the assertion that religious fanatics are very dedicated can be recognized as an argument because the claim that precedes it is so remarkable:

Religious fanatics are the best musicians in the world. They are very dedicated.

3.4   ADDITIONAL MEANS OF IDENTIFYING ARGUMENTATION

If the context provides no clues, other aids must be used to identify the arguments. It is in the interest of a person trying to resolve a difference of opinion that the listener or reader be able to interpret the argumentation correctly. It can be assumed that it is the speaker's intention to make the arguments recognizable as such. If this intention is not clear from the verbal context, then it may become clear if the broader, nonverbal context is taken into account. The specific *situation* in which something is said and the *cultural context* in which it happens sometimes clarify a lot:

> "The meeting hasn't started yet. Martin is coming down the hallway."
>
> "Thousands of homemakers use Andy!" (from an advertise-ment)

In the first example, the speaker asserts that the meeting has not yet started. Without knowing that Martin will be chairing the meeting, one would not realize that Martin's coming down the hallway is an argument justifying this assertion. In the second example, without knowing that the assertion is part of an advertisement, one could not guess that the widespread use of Andy is being used as an argument for buying it.

When interpreting argumentation, both general and specific background information can be important. A person who is not part of the intended audience may not have all of this background information. Sometimes the interpretation requires knowledge of a specific field. An example of this is a passage from an essay on discus throwing:

> In contrast to what you claimed in *Athletics Quarterly*, differences in air speed produce differences in air pressure. According to Bernouilli's principle, when the speed is highest, the pressure is lowest, and vice versa. The pressure (force per unit area) on the underside of the discus is higher than that on the upper side. As a result there is a lifting force (l) which is perpendicular to the velocity vector of the discus.

3.5   EXPLANATION, ELABORATION, AND CLARIFICATION

In interpreting argumentative discourse, one should start from exactly what the speaker or writer has said. Only when problems arise in the interpretation should other clues be considered. We must always guard against letting our own opinions influence our interpretation.

Even when the presence of an indicator seems to clearly mark something as an argument, it may still not be correct to interpret it as such. Particularly dangerous are *because* utterances, which often give causes rather than reasons. Instead of being arguments, such utterances serve to explain, elaborate, or clarify:

> The pudding didn't stiffen because I didn't put enough gelatin in it.

An important characteristic of explanation, elaboration, or clarification is that whatever is being explained, elaborated, or clarified is something that is already accepted. The situation is very different with arguments, which are always brought to bear on a standpoint that has not yet been accepted. This characteristic is sometimes exploited by speakers or writers; they may try to make their standpoint appear to be a statement of fact and their argumentation merely an explanation, thus creating the impression that their standpoint needs no defense:

> However painful it may be, social welfare must be cut. I shall attempt to explain that. We have been living beyond our means for many years and the high costs of the welfare state inhibit economic productivity.

Even when there is no conscious attempt at deception, it quite often happens that an utterance that seems on the surface to serve as some sort of explanation, on closer examination turns out to have a justifying or refuting function and must therefore be treated as argumentation. When in doubt, it is advisable to be cautious and to treat the explanation as an argument.

3.6 A MAXIMALLY ARGUMENTATIVE INTERPRETATION

To view borderline cases as argumentation is to follow the strategy of *maximally argumentative interpretation*. Any utterance that, for instance, might also be just a remark or an explanation is interpreted as argumentation. Being so charitable in cases where the argumentative function of an utterance is not really clear, but is nevertheless a realistic option, minimizes the risk that utterances important to the resolution of a difference of opinion will be overlooked in the analysis.

In the following essay on the design of banknotes, it is clear that the strategy of maximally argumentative interpretation is in the interest of everyone who sincerely wants a resolution of the difference of opinion. Both the writer—who thinks that Dutch banknotes are radically different from American ones—and the reader—who does not necessarily agree—benefit from a maximally argumentative interpretation of the sentence containing the italicized words:

> Dutch banknotes can easily be distinguished because of the clearly legible writing on them and the different colors and sizes for different denominations. In this respect Dutch banknotes are radically different from American dollars. *American banknotes are conspicuous for* their very uniformity: they all have the same size, the same general appearance, the same color, and only the numbers on them indicate the difference in value. You would think that this would cause a lot of mistakes, but experience has shown that Americans do not confuse their banknotes any more often than people in other countries do.

The strategy of maximally argumentative interpretation should also be followed in cases where no other meaningful interpretation is possible and where there is no reason to assume that the utterance is intended as nonsense:

> You'd better take an umbrella. Or do you want to get wet?

Taken literally, the question "Or do you want to get wet?" is absurd. Getting wet is not a realistic alternative. Generally speaking, everyone prefers not to get wet. So this cannot be viewed as an ordinary question. If one takes the speaker seriously, one must assume that the question is intended to indirectly convey something else, such as the assertion that "Otherwise you'll get wet" or "That's the only way to keep from getting wet." In a maximally argumentative interpretation, the question is viewed as an argument for the speaker's standpoint "You'd better take an umbrella." If the speaker is serious, this is naturally how the question is meant to be taken.

A discourse may contain a question that is seriously intended as such, of course, but in the absence of evidence to the contrary, in a context of disagreement the maximally argumentative interpretation should be chosen.

FURTHER READING

Along the same lines as the analysis propounded here, F. H. van Eemeren, R. Grootendorst, S. Jackson, and S. Jacobs explain in *Reconstructing Argumentative Discourse*, Tuscaloosa: The University of Alabama Press, 1993, how real-life discussions can be reconstructed in terms of a critical discussion. See also F. H. van Eemeren, R. Grootendorst, S. Jackson, and S. Jacobs, "Argumentation," in T. A. van Dijk (Ed.), *Discourse as Structure and Process. Discourse Studies: A Multidisciplinary Introduction*, vol. 1, London: Sage, 1997, pp. 208–229; C. W. Tindale, *Acts of Arguing*, Albany, NY: State University of New York Press, 1999, chapter 5; and F. H. van Eemeren and P. Houtlosser, "Rhetorical analysis within a pragma-dialectical framework: The case of R. J. Reynolds," *Argumentation*, 2000, vol. 14, no. 3, pp. 293–305. An overview of the state of the art in the development of interpretation and reconstruction methods is provided by M. A. van Rees, "Argument interpretation and reconstruction," in F. H. van Eemeren (Ed.), *Crucial Concepts in Argumentation Theory*, Amsterdam: Amsterdam University Press, 2001, chapter 7.

EXERCISES

1. Which of the utterances in the following passages are arguments? How can you tell? When in doubt apply the strategy of the maximally argumentative interpretation.
   a. I had to play the part of a scientist. Since I look rather intelligent, which by the way I am not, this was no problem at all.
   b. The employees' representatives had not taken the trouble to work out their proposal. This is hard to understand, considering that they are all experienced administrators.
   c. Can anyone explain why Douglas Hurd has been chosen to chair the Booker Prize judges? His own novels—mediocre political thrillers—have never been shortlisted for the Betty Trask Award, let alone for the Booker. And on the one occasion in his political career when he could have championed the cause of literature, he preferred to equivocate: As Home Secretary at the time of the fatwa he refused to meet Salman Rushdie, expressing a lofty disdain for both the novelist and the Ayatollahs. Of all his unpleasant duties at the Home Office, he once said, by far the worst had been reading The Satanic Verses.

      A few years ago I gave Rushdie a copy of Hurd's novel Send Him Victorious, hoping that he would return the insult with compound interest. No such luck: the next time I saw him, he told me he had found it quite unreadable.
   d. *An upgrade on cattle class*

      I enjoyed Matthew Engel on air travel (*Travel Sick*, February 14). At one stage, I travelled regularly around the Far East and found Cathay Pacific easily the most pleasant airline. They had the friendliest and most helpful staff. Unlike Engel, I never was offered oral sex, but then I never traveled first class. Cathay's planes were invariably half empty. By folding down the armrests on a row of seats, I could make a smashing bed.

      Could airlines not take a leaf out of the car manufacturers' book? There is a basic car, with optional extras such as electric windows, sunroof, central locking and heated seats at extra cost. You pay for what you get.

      I never watch the films on planes, and never eat the food (I take my own), but I would willingly pay more for extra legroom. I generally travel with only cabin baggage. Could not those who do this gain a reduction? After all, we are reducing an airline's costs. Give the passenger a bit of choice.

e. *Michael Heseltine:* "How can Britain flourish, if the unions are to be offered back the power to act as wreckers of the economy?"

f. John Major, struggling to patch together his crumbling European policy and his stumbling EC Presidency, will no doubt talk a lot about subsidiarity and the democratic deficit over the next few weeks and months. Well, I for one, will only believe Mr. Major's new commitment to subsidiarity when he puts into practice at home that which he recommends for Europe. I will believe him when he agrees to devolution and decentralization here at home. If it's good for Europe, why is it not good enough for Britain?

g. Winners set their daily goals the afternoon or evening before. They list on paper in a priority sequence at least six major things to do tomorrow. And when they start in the morning they go down the list, checking off the items they accomplish, adding new ones and carrying over into the next day's itinerary those they did not complete.

   What would happen if you did your grocery shopping without a list? You'd see all the packaged TV advertised displays, a potpourri of irresistible goodies and items. You'd be overwhelmed with goals you didn't set, didn't need and didn't want.

h. *Re "U.S. Recommending Strict New Rules at Nursing Homes"*
   To the Editor:
   The eight-year delay in the delivery of this report is explained by the need to analyze huge amounts of data from nursing homes around the country.

   Shouldn't the results be published and made available to consumers on a state-by-state basis, a national nursing home report card, if you will, so that families can make informed decisions about the best nursing homes to care for their loved ones?

i. *Cell Phone Hazards*
   To the Editor:
   In "Cell Phones and Safety" (editorial, July 19) you mention the debate 70 years ago about safety implications of car radios. Let this reader tell you that the only time he ran off the road was just five years ago—while changing stations on the car radio.

   Recently in downtown Greenwich, Conn., I watched an apparently healthy young man in business dress talking on his cell phone as he began to cross the street against the policeman's dictate to wait. Unhearing at first, he got the message 10 feet into the street and backed up still talking. Then, when the officer waved him across, he was further distracted by his conversation and had to wait again until traffic cycled through before he finally made it.

If walking is that difficult when using a cell phone, then its use when driving must certainly be outlawed.

j.   *The Pentagon's Anti-Gay Policies*

No amount of anti-harassment training can correct the injustice of the ban on openly gay service members in the United States military. Last week Defense Secretary William Cohen released yet another set of guidelines on how to stop anti-gay harassment. But this new action plan, like previous guidelines, will most likely prove ineffective because the "don't ask, don't tell" policy on which it is based is unworkable. The way to curb harassment is to allow gays to serve openly without fear of expulsion if they report harassment.

The policy adopted in 1993 was supposed to provide more humane treatment for gays by allowing them to serve if they did not disclose their sexual orientation or engage in homosexual conduct. It has instead forced gays to lie, and has resulted in more harassment and a near doubling in the numbers of people being discharged annually on the basis of homosexuality.

The new plan calls for more anti-harassment training and sanctions against those who engage in or tolerate harassment. But victims of harassment could still be ousted if they happen to disclose their sexual orientation in the course of making a complaint. This absurd situation forces victims who want to keep their jobs to suffer in silence.

Homophobia in the military today is undeniable. Even Mr. Cohen has said that anti-gay harassment seriously undermines discipline and order. The only real solution is for congress and the president to repeal the ban that was written into law in 1993 and that continues to fuel anti-gay bias.

4

Unexpressed Standpoints and Unexpressed Premises

*I*n argumentative discourse, it is quite common for premises or stand-points to be left unexpressed. Although not explicitly expressed, these implicit elements are indirectly indicated in the discourse. By openly and intentionally appearing to violate one or more of the communication rules normally followed by everyone who observes the Communication Principle, the speaker or writer conveys something more than the literal content of an utterance. With the aid of the Communication Principle, the communication rules, and some basic principles of logic, such indirectness can be understood, and specific types of indirectness, such as unexpressed premises and unexpressed standpoints, can be identified and reconstructed in the analysis.

4.1   IMPLICIT ELEMENTS IN ARGUMENTATIVE DISCOURSE

In practice, certain elements of argumentation are often left out. When this does not happen unintentionally and the omitted elements are implicitly present in the argumentation, then they are

49

called *unexpressed*. In the following discourse by the caretaker of a university building, the words in parentheses constitute an *unexpressed premise*:

> I wouldn't even consider getting a different job, because in most other jobs I wouldn't be able to bring along my dog Sherry (and I have to be able to bring Sherry).

Standpoints, too, can be unexpressed. In the following argument, the standpoint in brackets is only implicitly present:

> The world is full of suffering. If there were a God, there wouldn't be so much suffering. (Therefore, there is no God.)

Although one might think otherwise, the reason for omitting an argument or a standpoint is not always the intention to deceive others. Things are often left out of argumentation because they seem obvious. On the other hand, sometimes elements are left unexpressed in order to cover up the weakness of the argument. Take the following example:

> It is obvious that children should ideally be raised in a family with both a mother and a father, because it has been that way for thousands of years.

Here there is obviously an unexpressed premise. "It has been that way for thousands of years" can only be a justification of the standpoint "Children ideally should be raised in a family with both a mother and a father" with the addition of a statement like "Everything that has been done for thousands of years is good" or "If something has been done a certain way for thousands of years, then it is necessarily the best way." Because this additional element is implicitly present in the explicit argumentation, it is called an unexpressed premise.

Even though an unexpressed premise is not explicitly presented, it may still be criticized by the other party:

> I completely disagree. Why should something be good just because it's been done that way for a long time? Wars have been waged for thousands of years, but that doesn't prove war is good.

The protagonist in this case should have been aware of the weakness of the unexpressed premise. He or she could have anticipated the criticism by presenting argumentation to defend this unexpressed premise:

It is obvious that children should ideally be raised in a family with both a mother and a father, because it has been that way for thousands of years. And if something has been done a certain way for thousands of years, then it is necessarily the best way; it is the result of a process of historical selection.

These examples show that unexpressed elements, even though they are implicit, can crucially influence how the discussion proceeds and therefore also influence its outcome. Not only antagonists but also protagonists can pursue an unexpressed premise. Antagonists can also agree or disagree with an unexpressed standpoint that they have inferred from the reasons the protagonist has put forward.

In evaluating argumentation, unexpressed elements can be very important, particularly when evaluating the soundness of the argumentation. Therefore, when analyzing argumentation, it is important to note what elements in the argumentation have been omitted and to figure out carefully which statements need to be added to complete the arguments.

4.2 INDIRECTNESS AND THE RULES FOR COMMUNICATION

Unexpressed premises and unexpressed standpoints are examples of indirect language use that is typical of normal everyday speech. Indirectness means that the speaker says what he or she means in a roundabout way rather than in a direct way. Someone may say "Would it be too much trouble to take this package to the post office?" while also meaning to request that the listener do the job.

Indirectness is a special kind of implicit language use. The implicitness referred to here is quite different from a salesperson's saying "It's 170" instead of "I inform you that the price of that suit is 170 dollars." In this type of "ordinary" implicit language use, there is no attempt to convey something additional in a roundabout way.

In indirect language use, speakers not only mean to convey more than what they say, but also indicate this to the listener in their presentation. Otherwise, indirectness would not communicate anything. The big question, however, is how do speakers convey that they are saying something indirectly? How is one supposed to know that something different is meant from what is said?

In answering this question, it helps to realize that when people really want to communicate with each other, they follow the *Communication Principle*. According to this principle, people who are communicating with each other generally try to make their contributions to the communication match, as much as possible, the purpose of their communication. To do so, they must observe certain general *rules for communication*.

The most important rules are these:

1. Be clear.
2. Be sincere.
3. Be efficient.
4. Keep to the point.

The *clarity* rule is that whatever is said or written should be as easy to understand as possible. The *sincerity* rule is that it must not be insincere. The *efficiency* rule is that it should not be redundant or pointless. And the fourth rule, the *relevancy* rule, is that it must appropriately connect with what has gone before.

The communication rules are formulated here as if they were commandments, and so they are, for people who want to communicate effectively. Generally speaking, it can be assumed that everyone follows these rules most of the time. That is why it is immediately noticeable when someone does not. This is what speakers take advantage of when they want to convey something over and above the literal content of their words. By violating or appearing to violate one or more of the rules, yet at the same time not entirely abandoning the Communication Principle, they make it clear to the listener that they mean something different or something more than what they are saying. It is in this way that the Communication Principle and the communication rules give language users the opportunity to be indirect and to recognize indirectness in others.

4.3   CORRECTNESS CONDITIONS FOR SPEECH ACTS

The communication rules are, in principle, always applicable regardless of the function of an utterance. It makes no difference whether the speaker is making an announcement or a promise, explaining something, or defending a standpoint; in performing any of these various kinds of *speech acts*, the communication rules must be observed. What it means to observe these rules, however, varies according to which speech act is being performed. For a promise, the rule "Be sincere" requires that speakers must really intend to do what they promise. For a request, they must sincerely wish the listener to comply with their request. For each of the various kinds of speech acts, a more precise description can be given of what it means to follow the Communication Principle. This is done by formulating specific *correctness conditions* that each kind of speech act must meet.

Argumentation is also a speech act, and therefore certain conditions must be fulfilled for argumentation to be correct. As is the case for all speech acts, there are two main types of correctness conditions, namely, *preparatory conditions* and *responsibility conditions*. The preparatory conditions state what the speaker must do in order to follow the efficiency rule. For argumentation, this rule requires that it is part of the speaker's commitments not to undertake a redundant or pointless attempt to convince someone of a standpoint. The preparatory conditions state that the speaker must believe that the listener (a) does not already fully accept the standpoint, (b) will accept the statements used in the argumentation, and (c) will view the argumentation as an acceptable defense (or refutation) of the proposition to which the standpoint refers.

If the first condition is not met, the attempt at convincing the other party is redundant. If either of the other two conditions is not fulfilled, the speaker's attempt is pointless: It is not possible to convince someone by making use of an argument that is unacceptable to the other party. If the speaker is to be taken seriously, it must be assumed that these three conditions are met, unless there are clear indications to the contrary.

The responsibility conditions describe what the speaker must believe in order to follow the sincerity rule. For argumentation, this rule means that the speaker will try to convince the opponent without deceiving. The responsibility conditions that must be met for argumentation state that the speaker believes that (a) the standpoint is acceptable, (b) the statements used in the argumentation are acceptable, and (c) the argumentation is an acceptable defense (or refutation) of the proposition to which the standpoint refers.

If one takes the speaker seriously, one must assume that he or she meets these conditions, unless there are clear indications to the contrary. Otherwise, one would be unfairly accusing the speaker of deliberately attempting to mislead.

4.4 VIOLATIONS OF THE COMMUNICATION RULES

A speaker who complies with the Communication Principle normally tries to follow the communication rules, and a listener who observes the Communication Principle normally assumes that the communication rules are being followed. Problems arise when it appears that one of the communication rules has been violated without it being the case that the speaker has abandoned the Communication Principle. At this point, the charitable listener does not immediately assume that the speaker, through unclarity, insincerity, inefficiency, or pointlessness, has disrupted the communication for no good reason. Instead, the listener tries to interpret the speaker's words in such a way that the apparent violation acquires a plausible meaning. (We are not referring here to a slip of the tongue —or pen—or to any other unintentional violation.)

In practice, people find it difficult to recognize an obvious violation of the communication rules without immediately looking for an explanation that makes sense of the violation. If someone interrupts an animated conversation about a mutual friend's love life with the irrelevant remark "It's a little windy today," listeners are likely to interpret the remark as, for example, a warning that the friend is just coming into the room. Speakers can take advantage of this "rationalizing" tendency on the part of listeners and intentionally convey something more than they are literally saying by means of an open violation of one of the communication rules. This is exactly what happens in indirectness. Listeners know that it is happening because it is the only way to make sense of an obvious violation of the communication rules.

4.5   DIFFERENT FORMS OF INDIRECTNESS

All communication rules can be used to convey something indirectly, and violations of different communication rules lead to different forms of indirectness.

The clarity rule states that speakers must ensure that listeners understand what they mean; on the grounds of this rule, listeners can assume that it is possible for them to figure out the speakers' meaning. A promise expressed vaguely or unclearly can be interpreted as an indirect expression of reluctance or even refusal:

Gary: When are you going to fix that broken coffee grinder?
Mary: Sometime.

The sincerity rule states that the speaker must be sincere, and on the grounds of this rule the listener can assume that the speaker means what he says. By saying something obviously insincere, the speaker can ironically (and indirectly) convey the opposite of what he or she actually says:

> So you didn't even recognize your ex-boyfriend any more? He must have been flattered.

The efficiency rule states that speakers may not say anything that they know to be redundant or pointless, and on the grounds of this rule listeners can assume that whatever a speaker says is not flawed in these respects. By using obvious redundancy, a committee member who thinks the meeting time is being wasted on chit-chat can indirectly make clear that he thinks it is time to get down to business:

> I hereby open this meeting!

And a pointless question—because it has no answer—can be used to indirectly express a complaint:

> When will I ever find happiness?

The relevancy rule states that speakers must ensure that their statements are a suitable response to what has preceded them, and on the grounds of this rule, listeners can assume that this is the case. A response that obviously does not connect up with what has just been said can be used to convey that the speaker refuses to discuss the topic:

> Mary: How would you feel about inviting John to have supper with us sometime?
>
> Gary: I think I'll go look and see if there's a can of beer in the fridge.

In all these and other variants of indirectness, speakers choose not to say directly what they mean. In practice, this happens quite often. There are many possible reasons for this. It may be that they consider a question more polite than a direct request or command. It may be they are afraid of losing face if their suggestion is rejected. Perhaps they are trying to give the other person as much freedom as possible to form their own opinion. They may also think it more strategic not to express their intentions too openly. Whatever the reason, what they say has an indirect meaning. This meaning will only be understood if speakers ensure that their violation of the communication rules is noticed and correctly interpreted by the listener.

4.6   MAKING UNEXPRESSED STANDPOINTS EXPLICIT

Even if speakers do not explicitly express their standpoint, as a rule, they expect the listener to be able to infer this standpoint from the arguments put forward. Why would they otherwise bother to present argumentation?

When an argument lacks an explicit standpoint, it is not only immediately obvious that the standpoint is missing, but it is also easier than in the case of other indirect speech acts to figure out what is really meant. This is because there is an extra tool available, namely logic (see also chap. 6, section 3, this volume). All argumentation is based on reasoning, and if speakers are arguing sincerely, they do not believe that this reasoning is invalid. Only then can the argument be an acceptable defense or refutation of the proposition to which the standpoint is related. If a speaker knew in advance that his or her reasoning was not valid, then the argument would be pointless. A listener who takes the speaker seriously must assume that the latter has at least made an attempt to present valid reasoning.

In the simplest case, a defense consists of one single argument, which is based on one line of reasoning. If the standpoint being defended is unexpressed, then the conclusion of this line of reasoning will be missing, and listeners who take the argument seriously will assume that the reasoning is valid and will therefore, if possible, supply the missing conclusion themselves. In other words, they will try to formulate a conclusion that logically follows from the reasoning presented. In the following fragment of conversation, the sculptor being interviewed breaks off his sentence in the middle, indicating that he considers his listeners capable of supplying the conclusion themselves:

> The only good museum director is of course one who buys your work. If he doesn't do that, he's a real jerk. Now Mr. Bianchi has never bought anything of mine, so ...

It is easy to reconstruct the reasoning of this argument:

	1.	If a museum director does not buy my work, then he's a real jerk.
	2.	Mr. Bianchi has never bought any of my work.
Therefore:	3.	Mr. Bianchi is a real jerk.

This reasoning is *valid*; there are no holes in the logic. If one accepts statements 1 and 2, one is forced to accept the conclusion as well.

Therefore, assuming the sculptor does not intend to abandon the Communication Principle, "Mr. Bianchi is a real jerk" can be considered to be the unexpressed standpoint.

Similar cases can be resolved in the same way. First, one must determine what the logical conclusion would be. If there is more than one possibility, one should choose the standpoint that in the light of the context and background information is most in accordance with all the communication rules.

4.7   MAKING UNEXPRESSED PREMISES EXPLICIT

With the aid of the Communication Principle, the communication rules, and logic, unexpressed premises, too, can be made explicit. This is the way it is done.

Technically, argumentation where one of the premises is missing is invalid reasoning. Consider the following example:

Olga: Claus likes to yodel, because he comes from Tyrol.

By itself, the statement that Claus comes from Tyrol does not justify the conclusion that Claus likes to yodel. The reasoning is only valid if another statement is added to it. The statement that needs to be added can be found most easily by connecting the explicit premise to the standpoint by means of an "if … then …" statement. The explicit premise is filled in after the "if," and the standpoint after the "then":

If Claus comes from Tyrol, then he likes to yodel.

If this statement is added to the argument, then the reasoning is logically valid: If the premises are true, then the conclusion must necessarily be true. The reasoning as a whole then has the logically valid form of the type called *modus ponens:*

1.   If p, then q (If Claus comes from Tyrol, then he likes to yodel.)
2. p (Claus comes from Tyrol.)
Therefore: 3. q (Claus likes to yodel.)

In a constructive critical analysis of argumentation, the reasoning underlying the argumentation must first be made valid by supplementing it with an "if … then …" statement. However, that is not sufficient. The added statement is, in fact, merely a literal repetition of what was already implied by the other statements. This means that in this form, the added statement would be redundant and therefore a violation of the efficiency rule. There is no reason to assume the speaker is violating this rule. It is more plausible—and certainly more constructive—to attribute to the speaker a statement that is more informative and does not violate the efficiency rule. This may be done, for example, by adding one of the following statements:

a. Every Tyroler likes to yodel.
b. All Tyrolers like to yodel.
c. Tyrolers like to yodel.
d. Most Tyrolers like to yodel.

Next, one considers which of these statements best fits the verbal and nonverbal context of the argument, and can reasonably be attributed to the speaker. In this example, the statement "Tyrolers like to yodel" meets these requirements. There is no indication that the argumentation is concerned with how many Tyrolers like to yodel. It is simply suggested that it is typical of Tyrolers to like to yodel. Therefore, statement *c*, in the absence of other evidence from the context, is the best choice. If there is no evidence against the choice of this particular interpretation, then it can be viewed as the unexpressed premise. In the analysis of the argument, this unexpressed premise must then be added in parentheses to the original argumentation:

> Olga's standpoint is that Claus likes to yodel, because he comes from Tyrol (and Tyrolers like to yodel).

4.8   UNEXPRESSED PREMISES IN A WELL-DEFINED CONTEXT

Up to this point, it has been assumed that argumentation takes place in a context that is not well defined and that provides no specific clues as to how the unexpressed premise should be formulated. This is not always the case, however. The context may be so well defined that it demands a specific phrasing of the unexpressed premise.

One must be careful not to formulate the unexpressed premise too hastily or by relying on preconceived notions. Therefore, as a rule, it is best to start from the assumption that the argumentation takes place in a context that is not well defined—unless such a nonspecific interpretation is unfair to the speaker. In other words, if the nonspecific interpretation entails attributing to the speaker a violation of the communication rules, then one should check whether the context also allows another, more specific interpretation that does not entail a violation.

Suppose that Sally responds to an invitation from her friend Elaine to go with her to a party with the following argument:

> I don't think you should ask me to go with you to that party. Ronald and Marlene are in Portugal!

Without further information about the context, there is no apparent connection between the argument ("Ronald and Marlene are in Portugal") and the standpoint ("I don't think you should ask me to go with you to that party"). In such a case, the listener trying to identify the unexpressed premise can do little more than supplement the reasoning with an "if ... then ..." statement, so that at least the requirement of logical validity is met.

If more is known about the context, then a more meaningful statement can be formulated that is probably closer to the intention of the speaker and is therefore preferable. For instance, if Sally is known to be very sad because her boyfriend Ronald has gone on holiday with her friend Marlene, then the following formulation is possible:

> Someone who is disappointed in love can't be expected to want to go to a party.

FURTHER READING

More attention to this approach to the problems of identifying unexpressed premises is paid in F. H. van Eemeren and R. Grootendorst, *Argumentation, Communication, and Fallacies: A Pragma-Dialectical Perspective*, Hillsdale, NJ: Lawrence Erlbaum Associates, 1992, chapter 6. For somewhat different approaches see S. Toulmin, *The Uses of Argument*, Cambridge, England: Cambridge University Press, 1958, chapter 3; T. Govier, *Problems in Argument Analysis and Evaluation*, Dordrecht, the Netherlands: Foris, 1987, chapter 4; and D. Hitchcock, "Does the traditional treatment of the enthymeme rest on a mistake?," *Argumentation*, 1998, vol. 12, no. 1, pp. 15–37. An overview of the state of the art in the study of unexpressed premises is provided in "Unexpressed premises" by S. Gerritsen in F. H. van Eemeren (Ed.), *Crucial Concepts in Argumentation Theory*, Amsterdam: Amsterdam University Press, 2001, chapter 3.

EXERCISES

1. Make the unexpressed premise explicit in each contribution to the following conversation.

    A *Jane:*   Paul can't be at home because his car is gone.
    B *Ann:*   Well, he can't have gone to the swimming pool, because his swimming trunks are on the clothesline.
    C *Jane:*   All the same, he could have gone swimming: Thursdays is nude swimming.
    D *Ann:*   Well, since he's taken the car, he certainly can't be cycling.
    E *Jane:*   Even that's not necessarily the case, since he could have put his bicycle in the car.

2. Make the unexpressed premise(s) or standpoint explicit in the following argumentative texts.

    a. You've got to have hope. Otherwise life has no meaning.
    b. It was not our intention to use the same players in every production. Our plan was that each of us would act no more than twice, in order to give everyone a chance. But then again, I love to act, I was the coordinator, and power corrupts.
    c. I've got a bite! My float disappeared under water.
    d. Leo will soon be unemployed because he works in the accounting department and all the work in that department is going to be computerized.
    e. *Woman on telephone to husband:* "I think Leo and Trudy are at home because their line is constantly busy."
    f. *Mother to daughter:* "You are absolutely not going skiing, because your father and I were never able to do that when we were young."
    g. So when Lévi-Strauss fled to New York City to escape the Nazis (his grandfather was a rabbi), he began work at the New School for Social Research on a more theoretical sort of anthropology. "I prefer it because it requires less contact with fellow human beings!" he exclaims with a flash in his dark eyes.
    h. *Re: media causing violence in kids*
        Your logic is perverted. It's all the fault of capitalism. None of these problems exist in Cuba.

3. At a public meeting, two politicians are discussing a proposal to legalize abortion. Make the premises explicit that are left unexpressed in each of their arguments.

> *Politician 1:* The sanctity of all human life has always been a foremost principle of our party. The members of my party in this House will therefore vote against the proposal to legalize abortion.
>
> *Politician 2:* You are right to set such store by the sanctity of human life, but you cannot include a six-week fetus. And another point: what about the sanctity of the life of the mother who has become pregnant against her will?

4. Make the unexpressed premise(s) or standpoint explicit in each of the following comic strips:

   a.

WIZARD of ID

   b.

c.

5

*The Structure
of Argumentation*

*T*he simplest argumentation consists of just one single argument, but the structure of argumentation can also be much more complex. Multiple argumentation, for instance, consists of more than one alternative defense of the same standpoint. And in coordinative argumentation, several arguments taken together constitute the defense of the standpoint. Another complex argumentation is subordinative argumentation, with arguments supporting arguments. Through the use of indicators, the verbal presentation sometimes provides evidence to the analyst as to whether the argumentation is multiple, coordinative, or subordinative. Quite often, however, there are no such indicators; then it may be difficult to tell coordinative and multiple argumentation apart. When in doubt, for the sake of reasonableness, the analyst should opt for a maximally argumentative analysis and analyze the argumentation as multiple. By relying on a well-considered reconstruction of subordinative argumentation, it is sometimes possible, in a well-defined context, to arrive at a more specific formulation of elements that are left unexpressed than would otherwise be justified.*

5.1 SINGLE ARGUMENTS

The defense of a standpoint often consists of more than a single argument. Several single arguments can be combined and arranged in a number of different ways to form the defense of a standpoint. Argumentation can be evaluated only after it is clear how the arguments fit together. And it can only be determined what the structure of the argumentation is when it is understood how complex argumentation can be broken down into single arguments.

In the simplest case, a defense consists of one *single* argument, that is, an argument that in fully explicit form consists of two and only two premises. Usually, one of these is unexpressed, so that the single argument appears to consist of only one premise. A defense consisting of only one single argument is very common. The argument is often embedded in a larger discourse that is not primarily argumentative:

> In concluding this review of your accomplishments here over the years, Petrewsky, I would like to congratulate you on behalf of all of us on your 35 years with the company. We hope you will enjoy the rest of the day, together with your wife and children. You have earned a substantial gift, and we are proud to offer you this trip to Hawaii, *because you have worked very hard for it.* Bon voyage!

When the defense amounts to one single argument, the problem is not so much how to break it down into components as to identify that there is an argument in the first place. The argument has the simplest structure possible.

Nonetheless, in order to get a more complete picture of the argument, which will be necessary for the evaluation, it may be helpful to make explicit the premise that is so often left unexpressed in a single argument. This is especially true if the unexpressed premise is pursued later in the discussion. In the example just given, the unexpressed premise is something like "Hard work should be rewarded."

5.2 MULTIPLE, COORDINATIVE, AND SUBORDINATIVE ARGUMENTATION

The first type of complex argumentation is *multiple argumentation*. It consists of alternative defenses of the same standpoint, presented one after another. These defenses do not depend on each other to support the standpoint and are, in principle, of equal weight. Each defense could theoretically stand alone and is presented as if it were sufficient to defend the standpoint:

> You can't possibly have met my mother in Marks & Spencer's in Sheringham last week, because Sheringham doesn't have a Marks & Spencer's, and as a matter of fact she died two years ago.

In the second type of complex argumentation, *coordinative argumentation*, the arguments do not form a series of alternative defenses. Coordinative argumentation is one single attempt at defending the standpoint that consists of a combination of arguments that must be taken together to constitute a conclusive defense. The component parts of coordinative argumentation are dependent on each other for the defense of the standpoint. They can be dependent on each other in several ways. Sometimes they are dependent because each argument by itself is too weak to conclusively support the standpoint:

> The dinner was organized perfectly, for the room was exactly the right size for the number of guests, the arrangement of tables was well thought out, and the service was excellent.

Another way they can be dependent is when a second argument rules out possible objections to the first argument, thereby reinforcing it:

> We had no choice but to go out to eat, because there was nothing to eat at home and all the stores were closed.

One possible objection to the first argument, "There was nothing to eat at home," is that food could have been bought at a store. Putting forward the second argument, "All the stores were closed," prevents this objection from being raised.

Characteristic of the third type of complex argumentation, *subordinative argumentation*, is that arguments are given for arguments. The defense of the initial standpoint is made layer after layer, as it were. If the supporting argument for the initial standpoint cannot stand on its own, then it is supported by another argument, and if that argument needs support, then a further argument is added, and so on, until the defense seems conclusive. Subordinative argumentation may consist of many layers:

> I can't help you paint your room next week,
> because
> I have no time next week,

because

I have to study for an exam,

because

otherwise I will lose my scholarship,

because

I'm not making good progress in my studies,

because

I've already been at it for more than five years.

In subordinative argumentation, the speaker anticipates that certain parts of the argumentation will need further defense. The part to be defended then becomes a *substandpoint*, which is defended by means of *subargumentation*. This subargumentation, in turn, can contain a *subsubstandpoint*, which needs to be defended by means of *subsubargumentation*, and so on. Subordinative argumentation can be seen as a chain of reasoning where the weakest link determines the strength of the whole, regardless of the strength of the other links.

5.3   THE COMPLEXITY OF THE ARGUMENTATION STRUCTURE

Argumentation can be of greater or lesser complexity, depending on the number of single arguments it consists of and the relation between these arguments. The number of arguments that need to be advanced depends, among other things, on the nature of the difference of opinion that the argumentation is intended to resolve. Resolving a multiple difference of opinion naturally requires more than one single argument (albeit not necessarily complex argumentation). Each proposition to be defended or refuted requires at least one single argument, so if there are several propositions being defended or refuted, then in principle several single arguments have to be put forward:

> Although you may not agree, I thought Dickinson was a good president and Sanford was not, because Sanford was just a skilled bureaucrat, while Dickinson was a really creative politician.

If the difference of opinion is a mixed one, then more than one party must present a defense, each of which may consist of a single argument or of more complex argumentation:

Max: Sanford was a good president.

Ellen: I entirely disagree.

Max: He managed to push a huge budget cut through Congress and satisfy all objections, while at the same time the whole educational system got reorganized.

Ellen: All he did was to carry out other people's ideas in an unimaginative way, without adding a single original idea of his own. He made a mess of secondary school education, not to mention the damage he inflicted on university education—it hardly deserves the name any more.

The complexity of the structure of the argumentation depends on what objections it addresses or anticipates. If protagonists meet with or anticipate objections to certain parts of their argument, then they need to come up with argumentation to defend those parts with still more arguments, thereby creating subordinative argumentation:

Jacobs: Petrewsky could be let go, because he already has 35 years of service and he wouldn't mind.

Peters: What do you mean, he wouldn't mind?

Jacobs: Well, for quite a while now he has been talking about wanting to take it easy and this way he will get the chance to do that!

Peters: But is it really true that he wants to take it easy?

Jacobs: Yes, because he told me so himself.

The criticism or anticipated criticism being countered by argumentation does not always involve the content of the premises (as in the Petrewsky example), but may also relate to their justificatory power. The antagonist may accept a given premise, but still doubt whether it lends sufficient support to the standpoint. To counter such criticism, the protagonist may supplement the original argumentation with other arguments that directly support the standpoint, thus creating coordinative argumentation:

William: This is a lousy vacation house; there's not even a corkscrew here.

Ellen: Don't you think you're exaggerating a bit?

William: Yes, but there aren't any wine glasses either, the chairs aren't comfortable, and there's no fireplace.

The antagonist's responses or anticipated responses may lead the protagonist to put forward not only subordinative or coordinative argumentation, but also multiple argumentation. Because multiple argumentation consists of several alternative defenses of the same standpoint, each of which by itself should be sufficient, it might look like "overkill." One reason for giving additional arguments is if the protagonist anticipates that one or more of the attempts to defend the standpoint might be unsuccessful. If the argumentation is directed toward a large group of people, for instance, their responses may be quite diverse. That seems to have been taken into consideration by the Society Against Profanity in composing the text for a poster campaign:

> When we designed the poster for train stations, we thought we might need more than just the main slogan: "Missed the train? Don't swear!" Lots of people might wonder *why* they shouldn't swear. In response to this question, we gave three arguments that we thought most people would see something in. Naturally, *we don't expect each of these reasons in itself to be equally convincing to everyone.*

Acceptability is always a matter of degree: people accept things to a greater or lesser degree. This is another reason multiple arguments are given. The additional arguments may raise the level of acceptance. Too many arguments may of course have the opposite effect:

> I am not seeing her, because I hardly even know her. I'm not attracted to blonde women anyway. Besides, with all the budget cuts at work, I'm way too busy these days for affairs like that. And don't forget that I still love you very much.

When all is said and done, the structure of argumentation is determined by the choices of the protagonist. In some cases a protagonist may put forward one single argument, while in other cases the protagonist may use a whole series of single arguments. The way in which the various single arguments relate to each other and to the standpoint is reflected in the argumentation structure.

5.4 REPRESENTING THE ARGUMENTATION STRUCTURE SCHEMATICALLY

Complex argumentation can always be broken down into a number of single arguments. And that is exactly what happens when the argumentation structure is analyzed. To present the results of the analysis in a clear and concise way, use can be made of the schematic overviews in Figures 5.1, 5.2, 5.3, and 5.4.

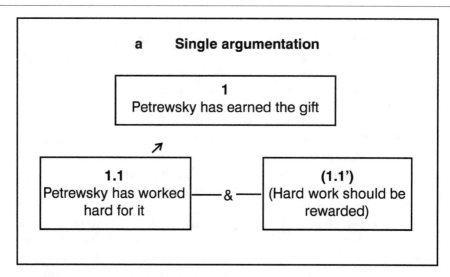

FIG. 5.1. Single argumentation.

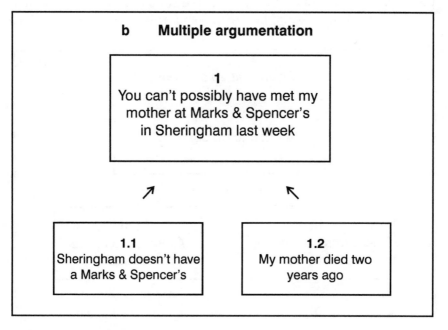

FIG. 5.2. Multiple argumentation.

A *single* argument is first assigned the number of the standpoint to which it refers (e.g., number 2), followed by a number of its own (e.g., 2.1). An unexpressed premise that has been made explicit is given in parentheses and is assigned a number followed by an apostrophe (') (e.g., 2.1'). The two parts constituting the single argument are joined by a horizontal line and an ampersand (&), and an arrow links the explicit premise to the standpoint advocated.

To show clearly that the arguments that form part of *multiple* argumentation all support the same standpoint, each argument is assigned the number of the standpoint followed by a number of its own: 2.1, 2.2, 2.3, and so on. Each separate argument has an arrow leading to the standpoint.

To show that the single arguments in *coordinative* argumentation have to be taken together in order to defend the standpoint, they are joined together with a brace and there is one single arrow linking the whole group to the standpoint. The relatedness of the single arguments is emphasized by linking them with horizontal lines and by assigning them all the same number, followed by a letter (2.2a, 2.2b, 2.2c, etc.).

Subordinative argumentation is indicated by the use of decimal points. An argument that has just one point (2.1 or 2.1a or 2.1') cannot yet be called subordinative. Subarguments are indicated by two points (2.1.1 or 2.1.1a or 2.1.1'); subsubarguments have three points (2.1.1.1), and so on. To emphasize that subordinative argumentation

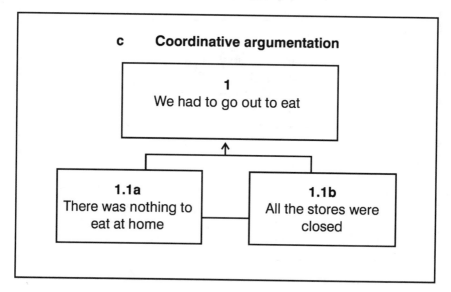

FIG. 5.3.   Coordinative argumentation.

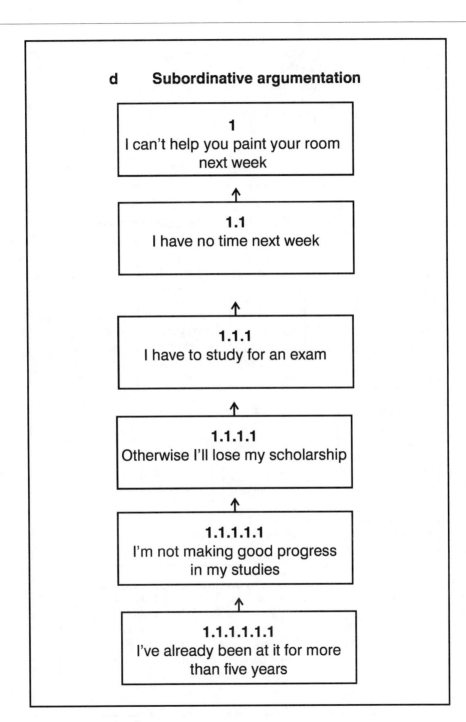

FIG. 5.4. Subordinative argumentation.

consists of a chain of arguments that are dependent on each other, they are represented in the schematic overview as a series of "vertically connected" arguments, linked with arrows.

Multiplicity, coordination, and subordination can also occur in combination, as is illustrated in Figure 5.5.

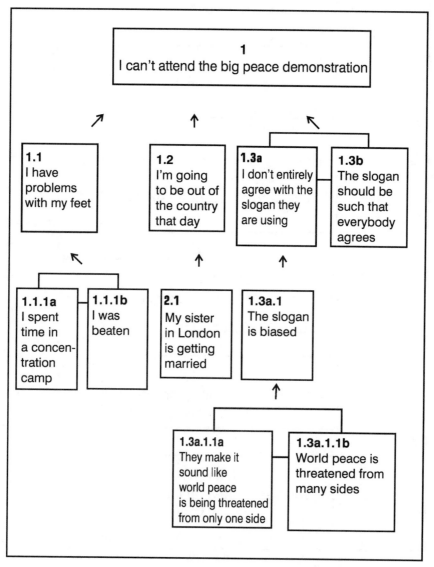

FIG. 5.5.   Combinations of various types of complex argumentation.

5.5   THE PRESENTATION OF COMPLEX ARGUMENTATION

In order to arrive at a reasonable evaluation of argumentation, its structure must be carefully identified: Is it single, multiple, coordinative, or subordinative, or even more complex?

The protagonist almost never explicitly indicates how the argumentation is structured. The following example is an exception to this; here the writer makes it immediately clear that the argumentation is not to be viewed as multiple but as coordinative:

> Why is the capital letter larger than the lower-case letter? There are six reasons for this, none of them conclusive in itself.

There are, however, certain words and expressions that may serve as indicators of the different types of structure. Indicators of *multiple* argumentation include *needless to say, in fact, apart from, not to mention, another reason for this is, one argument for this is, in the first place, secondly, by the way, incidentally, quite apart from,* and *aside from.* The following arguments use some of these indicators:

a   I don't see how you could have expected me to pick you up. *In the first place,* you have never even told me where you live. *In the second place* we didn't make any arrangement. *Not to mention the fact that* I would have had to leave work at least an hour earlier.

b   There's no way to decide whether winning a gold medal is due to talent or to training. *Aside from the fact that* talent is a very hard concept to define, some champions train a whole lot and others train very little. *Quite another argument is that* nobody has ever managed to say anything meaningful on this subject. *Apart from all this,* I would like to point out that the issue is wrongly put.

Indicators of *coordinative* argumentation include *as well as the fact that, in addition (to the fact that), on top of that,* and *don't forget that, especially because, even, plus, not only ... but also,* and *more importantly.* The following samples of argumentation use some of these indicators:

a   You should give me an allowance. *In addition to the fact that* I would like to buy lunch in the cafeteria, like all the other kids, it's a pain to always have to ask you for money for

school supplies. *And don't forget that* I have to save for enter-
tainment and presents for my friends.
b   You'd be better off studying English than French. *Not only* is
English more closely related to Dutch than French is, and
therefore easier to learn, *but* you *also* already know quite a
bit. *Plus the fact that* you hear English a lot more on television, so you know what it should sound like.

In *subordinative* argumentation, one argument is supported by another one, so that each supporting argument is really the beginning
of a new round of argumentation. The various arguments that form
part of subordinative argumentation may therefore be preceded by
any of the standard indicators of argumentation: *because, for that reason, therefore, after all, that is why, since, in view of*, and so on. If each of
the components of subordinative argumentation is marked by one of
these indicators, the argumentation structure is made much clearer:

> The Youth Center performs an important service for the com-
> munity. It fills the vital need for a place where young people
> can stay, *because* some young people don't have a home to go
> to, *because* their parents don't want them around, *since* they
> refuse to adapt their behavior to what their parents want, *be-
> cause* they find it suffocating.

Whereas there are very few indicators that are used exclusively in
subordinative argumentation, there are certain combinations of general indicators of argumentation that only occur with subordination,
for example, *for because, because because, because in view of*. These combinations occur surprisingly often in everyday speech:

a   I'd better not stay any longer, *for because* I'm so tired you
must find me boring company.
b   I think it is cool, *because because* the color is so bright it is
flashing.
c   Unfortunately you can't stay overnight at our place. *Because
in view of the fact that* my mother is staying with us, there's
not enough room in the house.

There are certain expressions for rounding off a complex argument
that tend to be used only with coordinative or subordinative argumentation, for example, *I conclude that, this follows from, in conclusion,
it follows from this that, taking everything into consideration, all things
considered I believe I am justified in saying that, ergo*. These expressions

are a little too pompous to be used for concluding a single argument, and they are not used with multiple argumentation.

One point of confusion is that some words—even some very common ones—are used to mark both multiple and coordinative argumentation. Examples include *and, also, and also, furthermore,* and *moreover.*

5.6   A MAXIMALLY ARGUMENTATIVE ANALYSIS

Coordinative and multiple argumentation are not always easy to distinguish from each other. Speakers rarely state which type of complex argumentation they are using, and indicators cannot always be relied on for clues either.

Sometimes the only way to tell whether the argumentation is coordinative or multiple is to go by the content of the arguments and the standpoint. In the following example, the content of *a* is clearly coordinative and that of *b* is clearly multiple:

  a I think we ought to buy this scarf, because it's nice and warm and we can always exchange it.

  b Of course you should buy that laptop. It's not all that expensive, and it's OK to be a little extravagant on something you work with every day, don't you think?

In *a*, the fact that the scarf can be exchanged is not in itself sufficient reason for buying it. Therefore, the two arguments clearly have to be taken together. In *b*, on the other hand, the two not altogether consistent arguments are easily seen to be alternatives, as the second argument obviously takes into account that the first argument ("It's not all that expensive") might not be accepted.

In some instances, it is not at all obvious whether each argument is intended as a separate defense of the standpoint or whether the arguments are intended to be conclusive only when taken together, as in the following example:

> The book was severely damaged during transport. There are scratches on the cover, and the first five pages are dog-eared.

If one of the single arguments in complex argumentation turns out to be unsound, then the consequences for evaluating the argumentation as a whole are quite different depending on whether the structure is coordinative or multiple. In multiple argumentation there is more than one line of defense so that if one is undermined, the others still stand and may still provide conclusive defense of the standpoint. In coordinative argumentation, there is only one line of defense so that if any part of it is eliminated, the whole defense is weakened or even destroyed.

Because it affects the rest of the analysis, it is important to determine as carefully as possible whether the argumentation is coordinative or multiple. In doing this, one must consider not only the verbal presentation with possible indicators and any other clues, but also the Communication Principle and the assumption that the speaker is making a serious attempt to resolve the difference of opinion.

In truly ambiguous cases, where there is just as much reason to choose the coordinative as the multiple analysis, it is preferable to opt for an analysis as multiple argumentation. This ensures that each part of the argumentation is judged on its own merits and that the strength of each single argument is duly examined. If each of several single arguments by itself is sufficient to defend the standpoint, then argumentation consisting of two or more such arguments must be unassailable. And if one of these arguments is undermined, it does not do irreparable damage to the defense. This approach—choosing to analyze the argumentation as multiple in case of ambiguity—is called (on the analogy of the strategy of maximally argumentative interpretation) the strategy of *maximally argumentative analysis.*

Coordinative and multiple argumentation are quite commonly found side by side:

> I'm not very satisfied with this book, because the price is way too high. Secondly, it's in French, whereas a lot more people could read it if it were in English. In the third place, I wasn't allowed to work on it.

This argumentation has the following structure:

1   I'm not very satisfied with this book.
1.1   The price is way too high.
1.2a   It's a French-language book.
1.2b   If it were in English, more people would be able to read it.
1.3   I wasn't allowed to work on it.

5.7 UNEXPRESSED PREMISES AND COMPLEX ARGUMENTATION

As explained in chapter 4, for argumentation that does not have a well-defined context, it is preferable when making unexpressed premises explicit to assume that for every incomplete single argument there is one unexpressed premise. When the context is well-defined, it is usually possible to further specify the unexpressed premise. It may even turn out that a whole chain of subordinative arguments was implied and can now be reconstructed.

Suppose that the popular singer Madonna is in a TV ad, surrounded by a group of attractive members of the jet set, and confides to the audience the following message:

> You should use Wonder skin lotion. I use it myself!

Clearly, something is unexpressed here. If we knew nothing further about the context of these utterances, we could let it go at assuming that the unexpressed premise has to be something like "Whatever Madonna does you should do too." But in this particular context we can do better. We know that Madonna is appearing in a TV ad and that she belongs to the jet set, some members of which we have just glimpsed. This background information allows us to come up with a more specific (and more complex) formulation of the unexpressed premise, leading to the following reconstruction of Madonna's argumentation:

1	You should use Wonder skin lotion.
1.1	Madonna uses Wonder skin lotion.
(1.1')	(Whatever Madonna does, you should do too.)
(1.1'.1)	(Madonna belongs to the jet set.)
(1.1'.1')	(Everything the jet set does, you should imitate.)

"Everything the jet set does, you should imitate" is the unexpressed premise that connects the unexpressed premise "Madonna belongs to the jet set" with the unexpressed substandpoint "Whatever Madonna does, you should do too." This is indicated by means of the two apostrophes (") following the numbering of this premise.

A person who had forgotten that Madonna belonged to the jet set (1.1'.1) would be reminded of it by the images in the TV ad. The TV ad provides a well-defined context. Without this context, the formulation of the unexpressed premise as "Whatever Madonna does, you should do too" (1.1') would be too free an interpretation. And without supplementing this unexpressed argument with the unexpressed subordinative argumentation needed to support it, the total argumentation would be robbed of the justification that this well-defined context provides.

In this example, the context is well defined because the TV ad in which the argumentation is set provides a clear background and because Madonna is a well-known personality. In other words, the clues are found outside the verbal presentation. But in other instances, it may be the verbal presentation (everything that is said) that provides clues, in which case we speak of a well-defined verbal context. In either case, when analyzing argumentation, all the clues in the context should be used. Generally speaking, the better defined the context is, the more specific the commitments that can be attributed to the speaker.

In this same way, unexpressed standpoints can sometimes be more specifically formulated. A variation on Madonna's example, in the same context, will illustrate this:

> I use Wonder skin lotion.

In an analysis of this utterance, the argumentation can be reconstructed as follows:

(1)	(You should buy Wonder skin lotion.)
(1.1)	(You should use Wonder skin lotion.)
(1.1')	(In order to use skin lotion you first have to buy it.)
1.1.1	Madonna uses Wonder skin lotion.
(1.1.1')	(Whatever Madonna does, you should do too.)
(1.1.1'.1)	(Madonna belongs to the jet set.)
(1.1.1'.1')	(Everything the jet set does, you should imitate.)

FURTHER READING

For more elaborated treatments of problems concerning the structure of argumentation, see F. H. van Eemeren and R. Grootendorst, *Argumentation, Communication, and Fallacies: A Pragma-Dialectical Perspective*, Hillsdale, NJ: Lawrence Erlbaum Associates, 1992, chapter 7, J. B. Freeman, *Dialectics and the Macrostructure of Arguments*, Berlin: Foris/Walter de Gruyter, 1991, A. F. Snoeck Henkemans, *Analysing complex argumentation*, Amsterdam: Sic Sat, 1992, and D. Walton, *Argument Structure: A Pragmatic Theory*, Toronto: University of Toronto Press, 1996. An overview of the state of the art in the study of complex argumentation is provided in "Argumentation structures" by A. F. Snoeck Henkemans in F. H. van Eemeren (Ed.), *Crucial Concepts in Argumentation Theory*, Amsterdam: Amsterdam University Press, 2001, chapter 5.

EXERCISES

1. Is the argumentation in the following examples coordinative, subordinative, or multiple?
   a. There are two reasons why Dutch drama is practically unknown internationally. In the first place, the subject matter of Dutch plays is not of universal interest, and in the second place, Dutch is not a widely spoken language.
   b. I must have made a pathetic impression on him. First I followed him to Central Africa, and after that, I even accompanied him on a six-month hiking trip.
   c. It is a remarkable country. There is no sunlight to speak of; nevertheless, there are 15 million inhabitants.
   d. Aunt Agatha thought the house should be condemned. It smelled like rotten fish everywhere and the staircase had collapsed.
   e. The team uniform has become a recurring theme in our meetings. In my opinion it is time to stop arguing about the team uniform and do away with it altogether for games we play away. For those matches it doesn't serve any purpose, since the team members wear numbers anyway.
2. Identify the structure of the argumentation given for the standpoints in italics in the following texts.
   a. *The criterion of Boultbee:*
      If the reverse of a statement is absurd, then the original statement is an insult to the intelligence and ought never to have been made. (Standpoint: *A statement, the reverse of which is absurd, must not be made.*)
   b. All the talk you hear about language deficiency is wholly based on social prejudices. In this lecture, I shall defend the proposition that *there is no language deficiency in children from the working class,* because language deficiency does not exist at all—not in anyone—and it even could not exist, neither here nor anywhere else.
   c. *He thought that she had acted wrongly*: she ought to have admitted that he was right, or ought to have said that she had not understood him.
   d. *Newspaper article on the murder of Billie–Jo Jenkins:*
      The foster father of Billie–Jo Jenkins was jailed for life last night after being convicted of her "horrendous" murder with an 18-inch tent peg, on what the trial judge described as compelling evidence.

Sion Jenkins, aged 40, the deputy headmaster, was found guilty of the 13-year-old's savage killing at the end of a 2-day trial. There were shouts of "you monster" and "bastard" from the school-girl's natural family seated in the public gallery. Two female jurors burst into tears. Billie–Jo's relatives hurled abuse and spat.

The schoolgirl's natural mother, Deborah Harry, sobbed quietly while her father Bill jumped to his feet and punched the air.

The judge, Mr. Justice Gage, told Jenkins: "It was a furious attack, the motive for which only you now know. That girl was in your care as a foster child. You yourself were a deputy headmaster at the time, a man in a position of trust and authority in respect of children. These base facts are sufficient to show *what a horrendous crime this was.*"

3. Analyze the argumentation structure of the following argumentative texts.

   a. *Health education authority:*

   It's never easy trying to find the right moment to tell your partner you want to use a condom. No matter how long the relationship. But leave it too late and it becomes almost impossible.

   Once you're completely naked you can become so physically and emotionally involved that you run the risk of not using a condom at all.

   Which means not only running the risk of an unwanted pregnancy, but also of contracting one of the many sexually transmitted diseases. Like chlamydia, gonorrhea and, of course, HIV, the virus which leads to AIDS.

   So why not say you want to use a condom while you've still got your underwear on?

   You're still in control of your emotions, yet it's now become clear to both of you that you want to have sex.

   What if your partner doesn't have one? Then carry some on you, just in case.

   Because if there's only one thing that's going to be worn in bed, make sure it's a condom.

   b. *Letter to the editor:*

   Polly Toynbee says child benefit can "be universally paid to all mothers, taxing it back from high-earning fathers." While this may perhaps be technically feasible, it would be thoroughly undesirable.

It would increase stress—where the mother lives with a man who is not the father of her child(ren) the tax would presumably be levied on the stepfather, who may already contribute more than he thinks fair to the upkeep of another man's child(ren).

Would it be levied only on husbands or on unmarried partners, too? If the former, it would penalize marriage; if the latter, is Polly Toynbee recommending that the Inland Revenue dispatch bedsheet and DNA inspectors to see who is living with whom?

Would it be levied only on top-rate taxpayers, or at all tax rates? If the former, it would severely penalize single-earning couples, whose joint income may be as low as half that of dual-earner couples where each partner is taxed only at the 23 per cent rate; if the latter, it would also magnify the unemployment and poverty traps.

There is a very simple solution: tax child benefit as the income of the recipient. According to the Inland Revenue, this would yield £700 a year, a figure which would rise insofar as mother's income rose.

c. *Parks and Plazas, the Urban Backyard*
To the Editor:
Re "New York Still Needs Patches of Green," by Thomas Balsley (Op-Ed, July 22):

As a cultural anthropologist who has spent 25 years studying the psychological, social and cultural importance of parks and plazas, I would like to offer even more evidence that we should be redesigning, not eliminating, urban public space.

From a 15-year study of Latin American plazas, I discovered that well-planned public space increases social tolerance through informal cross-class and cross-gender contact. Urban public spaces, in New York as well as in Mexico and Costa Rica, provide an important forum for ideas and values to be expressed and worked out.

In addition, many neighborhood parks serve as backyards for people of modest means. Reducing the opportunities for relaxation and solace makes very little sense when their needs are so great.

d. *A Tax That Seems to Hit a Nerve*
To the Editor:
Re "The Moral Sense in Estate Tax Repeal," by Alan Wolfe (Op-Ed, July 24):

It is surely true, as Mr. Wolfe suggests, that most American parents, like most parents everywhere, have a deep desire to help their children flourish. It is also true that Congressional Republicans have been trying to exploit that desire as a way of generating support for repeal of the estate tax.

Yet repeal would primarily benefit those who are already in an unusually good position to assist their children, even with the tax in place. And it would do nothing for those Americans who have not taken part in the recent prosperity, and who have no wealth to leave their children.

That is why many people—including many parents—oppose repeal of the estate tax. And it is why we should be wary of concluding, as Mr. Wolfe does, that repeal of the tax truly "corresponds to the basic moral instincts of most Americans."

e. *Letter to the editor:*

Your City Comment supporting the abolition of duty-free shopping is out of tune with majority politics and consumer opinion and ignores the facts.

Duty-free costs the taxpayer nothing and abolition would not in fact lead to any additional revenue for the Treasury—indeed, a detailed study by National Economic Research Associates (NERA) concludes that net government receipts could fall by £18 million a year. Other studies have produced similar results for the Netherlands, Ireland and France.

Duty-free is an internationally successful business; to abolish it within the EU only would leave EU operators at a competitive disadvantage.

Why should City Comment rely on an emotional viewpoint rather than face the facts about a successful industry which creates revenue, employs more than 140,000 people and benefits both the traveler and the economy as a whole?

f. *The Internet Can't Free China*
   By JAMES C. LUH

While the Senate holds back from voting on normal trade with China because of hesitation about Chinese nuclear help to Pakistan, the senators should take another look at another issue in the trade debate: the questionable argu-

ment that modern technology will force China to lib-   5
eralize its political system.

As the Chinese expand trade with the West and
make greater use of computers and the Internet, the
thinking goes, an unstoppable current of ideas will   10
spur political reform. "When over 100 million people
in China can get on the Net," President Clinton has
argued, "it will be impossible to maintain a closed
political and economic society." But will it?

The Chinese government will never squelch all dis-   15
sident voices on the Web, but because Internet communication relies on each person or computer having
a unique, traceable address, the authorities can find
ways to locate users and punish activities they don't
like. There is an active debate in the United States,   20
where political freedom is sacrosanct and individuals
are guaranteed due process of law, about the clash between citizens' civil liberties and corporations' innovations for protecting security or profits. Imagine the
implications in an authoritarian state.   25

China is already monitoring what goes out over
the Internet and identifying where messages come
from. Ask Huang Qi, if you can: authorities have de-
tained him since June 3 for operating a Web site about
human-rights abuses. Or ask Lin Hai, who served   30
prison time for sending some 30,000 Chinese e-mail
addresses to a dissident information service.

Even those who only read dissident sites, rather
than contributing to them, cannot be sure of safety.
Surfing the Internet appears untraceable on the sur-   35
face, but users unwittingly leave behind detailed
footprints, as evidenced by privacy concerns among
Internet users in this country. Chinese computer experts have plenty of tools and techniques at their dis-
posal to follow these footprints.   40

Then there is blocking and filtering technology. A
user can't get a single bit of digital information from
the Internet without connecting his computer to it, and
services that provide the connections can interpose
equipment or software that blocks certain types of traf-   45
fic or keeps users from reaching certain Web sites.

50   The Chinese government has already blocked disagreeable Western sites like The Washington Post and Amnesty International, but the censors have had difficulty identifying offending sites fast enough to block them all. It could solve that problem by adopting a strategy used by a number of American-based systems, like America Online's AOL@School service:

55   Block access to any Internet services not on a pre-approved list.

Business trends within China could also end up limiting the Internet's power there as a liberalizing force. Analysts of the industry think many Chinese will eventually connect to the Internet not with per-

60   sonal computers, as Americans typically do, but through devices like set-top boxes and mobile phones, which have cumbersome keyboards. Chinese who went online this way could shop or get government messages, but might find it difficult to send

65   e-mail or post opinions to a Web bulletin board.

As Western companies work to protect copyrights and enhance the security of information they collect, new techniques for control of Internet communication are being developed every day. Even if American com-

70   panies do not sell their innovations to China directly, the Chinese will be able to develop them on their own or buy them from other nations. The Internet won't be free in China until other influences force the country to lift its most insidious trade barrier: the ban on ideas

75   that threaten Communist Party rule.

SPECIAL ASSIGNMENT 2

a. Search for examples of multiple, coordinative, and subordinative argumentation in recent newspapers, journals and magazines.

b. Before the next meeting, students compare their examples in discussion groups. They try to reach an agreement on which of the examples presented by their fellow-students can indeed be considered as clear examples of the intended structures. They should mark those cases that they cannot agree upon, or that they find doubtful, so that they can present these examples for further discussion in the following class meeting.

SPECIAL ASSIGNMENT 3

a. Formulate a standpoint on an issue of your own choice, and make a case for this standpoint in which all three forms of complex argumentation occur. Give a representation of your argumentation in the way that has been explained in chapter 5.
b. Submit a copy of the representation of the argumentation to the instructor at the next class meeting.

SPECIAL ASSIGNMENT 4

Analyze the structure of the following text by making a schematic overview. Submit the overview to the instructor at the next class meeting.

In his article "Plagiarism: A rich tradition in science," editor John Lowell argues, referring to an article by Dr. P. Smith, that Copernicus was also guilty of plagiarism: it appears that he "forgot" to mention that Aristarchos of Samos (310–230 BC) had already arrived at a heliocentric theory. It is, however, 5 doubtful that Copernicus knew of this.

Kant spoke of heliocentricity as a Copernican revolution: it is directly contrary to "common sense" (after all, we can see that the sun rises in the east and sets in the west), and more importantly, to a centuries-old geocentric, Christian-Scientific tradi- 10 tion. Copernicus needed all the support he could muster for his theory, and cited a great many classical writers to that end.

The fact that Copernicus did not refer to Aristarchos is not easy to understand, if he had, indeed, known him to be the intellectual author of heliocentricity. However, the best source 15 for Aristarchos' theory was Archimedes' *Sand reckoner*, which did not "appear" until 1544, a year after Copernicus' death. Another source, in which Aristarchos is vaguely cited, was possibly only consulted by Copernicus *after* he had already announced his hypothesis. 20

In conclusion, it can be said that the accusation that Copernicus committed plagiarism is at the very least doubtful and is

probably incorrect. In order to avoid being justly accused of something similar, I will mention now that my most important
25 source was: O. Gingerich, "Did Copernicus owe a debt to Aristarchos?" in *Journal for the History of Astronomy* 16, 1985.

SPECIAL ASSIGNMENT 5

Give an analysis of the text "Why Not Dutch?" by answering questions 1–4. The assignment should be handed in at the next class meeting. In the following class meeting, the instructor will discuss the assignment; the students will receive individual comments on their assignments.

1. Which proposition(s) is (are) the bone of contention in the text? Which roles do the parties in the dispute assume? Of which type is the dispute?
2. State precisely (by referring to line numbers) how the dialectical stages are represented in the text.
3. Give a schematic overview of the argumentation structure of paragraph 2-4. Explain why you think this is the correct analysis. N.B. Unexpressed premises need only be made explicit if they are supported by the author.
4. Make the unexpressed premise explicit in the following argument:

The proper place for acquiring knowledge of languages is at secondary school. After all, this is where a thorough instruction in foreign languages ought to be provided.

WHY NOT DUTCH?
Céline van Lier

The University of Amsterdam has recently revealed a plan to give a quarter of all lectures in foreign languages. The university gives two reasons for this in its Public Development Plan IX: on the one hand, the opportunity is created for foreign stu-
5 dents to follow a well-rounded programme in each of the Amsterdam faculties and, on the other hand, it provides a broadening of education for Dutch students at the University of Amsterdam, as a result of which, their position on the international labor market will be strengthened. I do not believe,

however, that giving lectures in a foreign language is wise. I 10
think I can show that I have a strong case.

Firstly, I am of the opinion that it is neither desirable nor
even necessary to make education more attractive to foreign
students. After all, it goes without saying that by attracting
large numbers of foreign students, the quality of education 15
will decline. The accessibility of education will be reduced
when this is followed (and given) in a language that is not the
native tongue of students and teachers. No one commands a
language quite as well as he does his native language and,
therefore, the transfer of knowledge will be impeded. In addi- 20
tion, most faculties already have to contend with an enormous
surplus of students.

In addition to the question as to whether or not this will be
to the detriment of the quality of education, there is also the
question as to whether it is not possible at the moment for for- 25
eign students to follow a well-rounded programme. The answer to this question is yes; if, at least, they first follow a Dutch
course (provided entirely by the University of Amsterdam).
And it is better to maintain this situation. For what is more
just; that thousands of Dutch students have to put up with lec- 30
tures in a foreign language, or that a handful of foreign students have to take the trouble to learn the language of their
country of residence?

Secondly, I believe that it is better to improve the competitive position of Dutch students in a different way. The proper 35
place for acquiring knowledge of languages is at secondary
school. After all, this is where a thorough instruction in foreign languages ought to be provided. If the universities start
teaching such basic skills, then the next obvious step is that
arithmetic and writing will also form part of the curriculum. 40

To summarize, it can be said that giving lectures in foreign
languages will be to the advantage of no one. It is not
far-fetched to suppose that this plan is nothing more than a
prestige object for the University of Amsterdam. The fact that
no one hesitates to exclude our own Dutch language from the 45
university may be called astonishing. Did not Simon Stevin[1]
once say that the Dutch language in particular was eminently
suited to academic work?

---

[1]Simon Stevin is a famous Dutch 16th-century mathematician.

II

Evaluation

6

The Soundness
of Argumentation

*W*hen evaluating argumentation, the argumentation must
first be checked for logical and pragmatic inconsistencies.
Then each individual single argument must be assessed to
determine whether it is based on valid reasoning. To do this, any unexpressed elements must be made explicit. Because the unexpressed premise is
usually also a clue to what type of argumentation is being used, it indicates
which argument scheme links the explicit premise to the standpoint. This is
helpful when evaluating the soundness of each single argument: then it
must be determined whether the constitutive argumentative statements are
acceptable and whether all the critical questions can be answered that are
relevant for the argument scheme that is used.

6.1   EVALUATING ARGUMENTATIVE DISCOURSE

Argumentative discourse can be defective in various ways. There
may be contradictions in the argumentation as a whole, and individual arguments may be unacceptable or otherwise flawed. To assess

the soundness of the argumentation and to determine whether the standpoint has been conclusively defended, one must first check for such weaknesses.

The evaluation of argumentation should be based on a solid analysis. The unacceptability of one part of multiple argumentation, for instance, has quite different consequences for the overall judgment than the unacceptability of part of coordinative or subordinative argumentation. For subordinative argumentation, one weak link in the chain of arguments undermines the strength of the whole. For coordinative argumentation, the result is that the whole defense is weakened. For multiple argumentation, however, the rest of the defense still stands, so there is a good chance the defense will still be conclusive.

To assess the soundness of argumentation, all complex argumentation must be broken down into single arguments, each of which must be assessed. It is advisable, however, not to proceed to the assessment of the individual arguments before determining whether the argumentation as a whole is consistent.

Inconsistencies in argumentative discourse are of two kinds: logical and pragmatic. A *logical inconsistency* is when statements are made that, because they contradict each other, cannot possibly both be true. For example, as pointed out by a psychologist in a newspaper review of two articles about "androgology," it cannot be true that this branch of social work is both a profession in which people actively try to influence their clients' behavior and a profession in which people do not try to influence their clients' behavior. The reviewer merges the views of both articles into one (multiple) argument and claims that they logically contradict each other:

> Last week's *Open Forum* magazine has two articles defending the importance of androgology. What exactly is androgology? The objective of this academic discipline is to improve the competence of social workers. Who are social workers? According to one of the articles, they are people who actively *try to influence* the behavior of the disadvantaged children they work with. According to the other article, they are people who *do not try to influence* their clients' behavior. So what, then, is androgology? It remains a mystery to me.

When argumentation contains two statements that, although not logically inconsistent, have consequences in the real world that are contradictory, it is called a *pragmatic inconsistency*. The promise "I'll pick you up in the car" does not in a strict sense logically contradict the statement "I don't know how to drive," but in everyday conversation, it is unacceptable for such a promise to be followed by this statement. Making the promise is not consistent with the statement.

Another example of pragmatic inconsistency was discussed in a newspaper article, describing a debate between two politicians, Felix Rottenberg and Elco Brinkman:

> Rottenberg didn't come off well in this debate as far as the internal consistency of his remarks goes, because he repeatedly attributed the views of his opponent Brinkman to Brinkman's family background. Rottenberg did this so often that at one point Brinkman said angrily, "Leave my father out of this." How can Rottenberg criticize the family-oriented party line of the Christian Democrats and at the same time keep on assuming that someone's views derive primarily from the atmosphere of their childhood home?

After any logical and pragmatic inconsistencies have been identified, the assessment of the individual single arguments that make up the argumentative discourse can begin.

The soundness of each of these single arguments, which are all intended to contribute to the defense of the standpoint, is judged by what they contribute to increasing the acceptability of the standpoint. In other words, each single argument must be judged according to the degree to which it justifies (or refutes) the proposition to which the standpoint refers.

To be considered sound, a single argument must meet three requirements: Each of the statements that make up the argument must be acceptable; the reasoning underlying the argument must be valid; and the "argument scheme" employed must be appropriate and correctly used.

6.2 THE ACCEPTABILITY OF ARGUMENTATIVE STATEMENTS

The acceptability of argumentative statements is easier to determine in some instances than in others. There are statements whose acceptability can be established with no problem. Examples of these are factual statements whose truth can be verified—for example, by consulting an encyclopedia or other reference work, by carrying out a simple experiment, or simply by careful observation:

> Pailleron was a nineteenth-century French dramatist.
> A palindrome is a word that can be read backwards as well as forwards.

"Level" is a palindrome.

Porcelain is very fragile.

My desk is dark gray.

Tommy, the cat, weighs exactly six pounds.

The acceptability of nonfactual statements can also sometimes be agreed on quickly, for instance, when they concern commonplace values or judgments:

Parents should take care of their children.

You shouldn't give up when your goal is in reach.

Good quality is always superior to junk.

Of course, in many other instances it is very difficult to agree on the acceptability of a statement, particularly if it involves a complex matter or is strongly tied to particular values and norms:

Reading is the best way to improve your language skills.

Breast-feeding is preferable to bottle-feeding.

In many instances cancer is caused by stress.

A man shouldn't be pushing a baby carriage.

It's good for the child if the mother works.

It's not good for the child if the mother works.

If such statements are not supported by further argumentation, the speaker's argumentation as a whole may not be accepted as an adequate defense (or refutation) of the standpoint. When evaluating argumentation, special attention should be paid to statements like these that are not supported by further argumentation. It might be the case that the audience has accepted them already at an earlier stage, or accepts them as they are, without any further support. Then they do not pose an acute problem to the parties involved in the difference of opinion. They may, however, be regarded as a problem by an outside critic who reflects more carefully on the argumentation. This problem can only be solved by gathering independent evidence. When the available time and opportunities are limited, this is not always feasible.

6.3   THE VALIDITY OF THE REASONING

A single argument can be considered sound only if the underlying reasoning is logically valid or can be made valid. If the underlying reasoning is logically invalid, then the argument is not an acceptable defense or refutation.

There is only one situation in which a single argument cannot be reconstructed as being based on valid reasoning, and that is if invalid reasoning is put forward explicitly. Reasoning that is incomplete can almost always be completed in a way that renders it logically valid. If a premise has been left unexpressed, the solution is simply to add to the argument the appropriate "if ... then ..." statement. However odd the resulting statement may be, the reasoning is valid.

It seldom happens that invalid reasoning is put forward explicitly. The result seems forced, as in the following example:

	1	If there is a God, then I will have a healthy baby.
	2	God doesn't exist.
Therefore:	3	I will not have a healthy baby.

The form of this invalid reasoning departs from the standard "if ... then ..." logical argument forms known as *modus ponens* and *modus tollens*.

a	*modus ponens:*	
	1	If ___ , then ...
	2	___
Therefore:	3	...

b	*modus tollens:*	
	1	If ___ , then ...
	2	Not ...
Therefore:	3	Not ___

Reasoning of the form of *a* or *b* is valid, regardless of how the dots and dashes are filled in, as long as exactly the same thing is filled in both times for the dots and for the dashes. There must be no deviation from the proper form, such as that seen in the "God doesn't exist" example.

6.4 THE USE OF ARGUMENT SCHEMES

The fact that a single argument is based on valid reasoning does not necessarily guarantee that the argument is conclusive as a defense or refutation. The soundness of the argumentation also depends on how it employs one of the possible argument schemes. By means of the *argument scheme*, the arguments and the standpoint being defended are linked together in a specific way, which may or may not be done correctly.

There are three main categories of argument schemes, and they characterize three different *types of argumentation*. For each type of argumentation, there is a particular relation between the argumentation and the standpoint. Compare the following three arguments:

1	Herman is a real man.
1.1	Herman is macho.
(1.1′)	(Being macho is characteristic of real men.)
2	A lottery for entrance to the university is absurd.
2.1	A lottery is not used to determine who gets to participate in the Olympic games either.
(2.1′)	(At universities the same standards apply as in sports.)
3	Ronald's headache will go away now.
3.1	He just took two aspirins.
(3.1′)	(Aspirins make headaches go away.)

These arguments each represent a different type of argumentation. This becomes clear if one considers the unexpressed premises. As shown in chapter 4, unexpressed premises are more informative than the conditional "if ..., then ..." statements in the logical argument forms known as *modus ponens* and *modus tollens*. In particular, they provide more information about the type of connection between the explicit reason and the standpoint. In the first argument, the argumentation is linked to the standpoint by claiming that one thing (being macho) is *symptomatic* of another thing (being a real man). In the second argument, an *analogy* is made between one thing (sports) and another (universities). In the third argument, one thing (taking aspirins) is presented as being the *cause* of another (the headache going away).

For each type of argumentation, different criteria of soundness are applicable. To determine whether a given argument meets the criteria relevant to that type of argumentation, certain critical questions must be asked. For an adequate evaluation, it is thus essential to carefully distinguish the main types of argumentation and to ask the right set of critical questions.

6.5   ARGUMENTATION BASED ON A SYMPTOMATIC RELATION

In argumentation based on a symptomatic relation, a standpoint is defended by citing in the argument a certain sign, symptom, or distinguishing mark of what is claimed in the standpoint. On the grounds of this concomitance, the speaker claims that the standpoint should be accepted:

> Jack is an experienced teacher, because he spends hardly any time on lesson preparation. (And little time spent on lesson preparation is characteristic of experienced teachers.)

Whether the trait mentioned in the argument is presented as typical of a certain group, as characteristic of a certain situation, or as an inherent quality of a certain personality, in all these cases, the defense employs an argument scheme based on a symptomatic relation. According to this presentation, one thing implies the other.

In the previous example, the fact that Jack spends little time on lesson preparation is presented as a sign of his teaching experience. The explicitized unexpressed premise makes clear that the relation between the argumentation and the standpoint is one of concomitance: "Little time spent on lesson preparation is characteristic of experienced teachers."

In evaluating the argumentation for the standpoint that Jack is an experienced teacher, not only must it be established whether it is indeed true that Jack spends little time on lesson preparation, but also whether the symptomatic relation is as strong as is suggested. An important question to ask is whether experienced teachers are the only teachers who spend little time on lesson preparation. In other words, are there not also other teachers who spend little time preparing their lessons? If there are, for instance, certain groups of inexperienced teachers who also spend little time on lesson preparation, then Jack's limited preparation is not necessarily a sign of his experience but may just as well be evidence of something else. His limited preparation may, for example, be a sign of laziness. Another relevant question is whether it is really generally true that experienced teachers spend little time on lesson preparation. Aren't there also experienced teachers who spend a lot of time preparing their lessons?

The general argument scheme for the symptomatic relation, of which the Jack example is a specific case, is:

> Y is true of X,
>
> *because:* Z is true of X,
>
> *and:* Z is symptomatic of Y.

The most important critical questions to ask about argumentation based on a symptomatic relation are:

- Aren't there also other non-Y's that have the characteristic Z?
- Aren't there also other Y's that do not have the characteristic Z?

Note that the same relation of concomitance can be used in the *opposite direction* as well, by mentioning the symptom in the standpoint rather than in the argument. The argument about Jack could have taken the following form:

> Jack hardly spends any time on lesson preparation, because he is an experienced teacher. (And experienced teachers spend little time on lesson preparation.)

Argumentation based on a symptomatic relation may occur in various ways. Something done by somebody can, for instance, be presented as *typical* of his or her character ("Sarah is a bitch: She almost exploded when she heard that Leah did pass her exam"). A certain phenomenon can also be presented as a *symptom* or a *sign* of something more general ("The behavior of the hooligans makes clear that our society has become much more violent"). Another case of argumentation based on a symptomatic relation is argumentation by *example*. Then a generalization is made, or a rule is introduced, by presenting a number of separate cases as indicative of something general:

> When people are over fifty this does not mean that their emotional life has become less active or has even disappeared. Romantic feelings can govern our life until we are very old. Did Picasso at the end of his life not write splendid letters to his young lover and did Richard Strauss not create his most lyrical songs when he was already over eighty?

In the case of argumentation by example the evaluation becomes more specific: It has to be established whether the cases mentioned as examples are indeed representative and whether they are sufficient to justify the generalization.

A *definition* too can connect a reason with a standpoint by way of a symptomatic relationship. Mary Steckel, for one, argues in this way that a speech made by the American politician George Bush displays exactly the features of postmodernism which he disapproves of:

> Not only consists the speech mainly of quotes, the speech is also stylistically awkward, eclectic and a-historic; the speech manifests a loss of depth and meaning, to mention just a few other definitions of postmodernism.

6.6 ARGUMENTATION BASED ON A RELATION OF ANALOGY

In argumentation based on a relation of analogy, a standpoint is defended by showing that something referred to in the standpoint is similar to something that is cited in the argumentation, and that on the grounds of this resemblance the standpoint should be accepted:

> It's not at all necessary to give James 10 dollars allowance, because his brother always got just 5 dollars a week. (And the one child should be treated just as the other.)

Whether the case or circumstance mentioned in the argument is presented as an analogue, as a model to be imitated, or even as an example to be avoided, in all these cases the defense makes use of an argument scheme based on *analogy*. The defense argues that what is true for the one case is true for the other case.

In the previous example, in order to argue plausibly that it is not necessary to give James 10 dollars allowance, implicit reference is made to the comparability of the two brothers and therefore to the equal rights of the two brothers with respect to allowance. The explicitized unexpressed premise makes clear that the relation between the argumentation and the standpoint is one of analogy.

To assess the soundness of the argumentation for the standpoint that it is not necessary to give James 10 dollars allowance, it must be determined whether the cases being compared really are comparable. Is there no significant difference between the cases being compared that might invalidate the comparison? For example, opinions on what is a reasonable allowance for a child may have changed over the course of time. If so, a different comparison, for example with other children the same age, may be more appropriate than a comparison with siblings.

The general argument scheme for the relation of analogy, of which the allowance example is a specific case, is:

$$Y \text{ is true of } X,$$
because: $\quad Y \text{ is true of } Z,$
and: $\quad Z \text{ is comparable to } X.$

The most important critical question to ask about argumentation based on analogy is:

- Are there any significant differences between Z and X?

Such differences can be pointed out in two ways: by claiming that Z has a certain characteristic that X does not have, or vice versa. Both forms of criticism are serious charges because basing argumentation on a relation of analogy assumes that X and Z share *all* characteristics relevant to the argument.

In fact, only if a comparison is drawn between the way in which matters relate in one area and the way in which matters relate in an entirely different area—so that the comparison that is made is a *figurative comparison*—is the analogy a real analogy in the strict sense. A funny example is the following reaction to a pronouncement made by Somerset Maugham that people who reread books are not very clever. After having first made some "ordinary" comparisons, the author uses an argumentation by analogy by making a comparison between never rereading a beautiful book and not enjoying a beautiful view for a second time:

> Why not reread a book that you like now and again? Doesn't one also look at the same paintings again and again? And doesn't one listen to the same music all the time? Maugham resembles the person who has a room with a beautiful view and decides to have the window plastered with paint after having looked out of it once or twice.

Unlike in the case of a *literal comparison*, when evaluating a figurative comparison, it makes no sense to investigate whether the concrete properties compared are indeed similar because they typically stem from different domains, which cannot be equated in this way. Instead, one should try to establish whether the two cases are similar on a more abstract level of comparison. By which general principle are the two connected and does this principle indeed apply?

6.7   ARGUMENTATION BASED ON A CAUSAL RELATION

In argumentation based on a causal relation, a standpoint is defended by making a causal connection between the argument and the standpoint, such that the standpoint, given the argument, ought to be accepted on the grounds of this connection:

> Lydia must have weak eyes, because she is always reading in poor light. (And reading in poor light gives you weak eyes.)

Whether the argument presents something as a cause of the effect that is mentioned in the standpoint, or as a means to an end, or as an action with a certain effect, in all these cases the defense makes use of an argument scheme based on a *causal relation*. In this presentation, it is suggested that the one thing leads to the other.

In the example just given, reading in poor light is presented as the cause of the claimed circumstance that Lydia has weak eyes. The explicitized unexpressed premise makes clear that the relation between the argumentation and the standpoint is a causal one.

To assess whether this argumentation is conclusive, the analysis must verify whether reading in poor light indeed always results in weak eyes. Perhaps the two things are unrelated, or under certain conditions the predicted result does not occur. Perhaps Lydia's eyes are so strong that reading in poor light does not harm them at all.

The argument scheme for a causal relation, of which Lydia's case is an example, is:

> Y is true of X,
> *because:* Z is true of X,
> *and:* Z leads to Y.

The most important critical question to ask about causal argumentation is:

- Does Z always lead to Y?

Just as in argumentation based on a symptomatic relation, causal argumentation can also be made in reverse order, whereby the argument mentions the effect and the standpoint the cause:

> Lydia must have read a lot with poor light, because she has weak eyes.

Where this variation in reverse is used, a second critical question can be asked, namely: Could the effect (weak eyes) have been caused by something else (something other than reading in poor light)?

A subtype of causal argumentation, in which the argument refers to an effect of what is mentioned in the standpoint, is *pragmatic argumentation*. This is when the standpoint recommends a certain course of action and the argumentation consists of summing up the favorable consequences of adopting that course of action:

> Doctors should go back to wearing white jackets, because this will create distance (and it is a good thing to have a certain distance between the doctor and the patient).

Of course, pragmatic argumentation can also be used to advise against a certain course of action:

> Doctors should stop wearing white jackets, because this will create distance (and it is not a good thing to have distance between the doctor and the patient).

In addition to answering the critical questions for causal argumentation in general, when evaluating pragmatic argumentation, one also has to determine whether the consequences mentioned in the argumentation are indeed favorable—or unfavorable, as the case may be.

6.8   THE PRESENTATION OF DIFFERENT TYPES OF ARGUMENTATION

Before argumentation can be evaluated by asking the critical questions that are relevant for the argument scheme employed, the argumentation must first be identified as argumentation of that specific type. Sometimes it is easy to determine the type of argumentation because of the presence of certain expressions that indicate what the relation is between the argument and the standpoint. In the following examples, the italicized expressions are signs of a symptomatic relation:

> Steven is a real adolescent, because he is terribly rebellious; and
> - *It is characteristic of* adolescents that they are rebellious.
> - *It is typical of* adolescents to be rebellious.
> - *It's natural for* adolescents to be rebellious.
> - *The way* adolescents *are is* that they are rebellious.
> - Rebelliousness *is typical of* adolescents.
> - Adolescents *are* rebellious.

An analogy may be signaled by any of the following expressions:

> The movement towards democracy of the 1960s was bound to fail, because the French revolution also failed; and
> - The movement towards democracy of the 1960s *is like* the French revolution.
> - The movement towards democracy of the 1960s *is comparable to* the French revolution.
> - The movement towards democracy of the 1960s *is similar to* the French revolution.

- The movement towards democracy of the 1960s *corresponds to* the French revolution.
- The movement towards democracy of the 1960s *is related to* the French revolution.
- The movement towards democracy of the 1960s *is reminiscent of* the French revolution.

A causal relation may be signaled by any of the following expressions:

Harry must have been drunk, because he drank a whole bottle of whiskey; and
- Drinking a whole bottle of whiskey *has the inevitable result that* you get drunk.
- Drinking a whole bottle of whiskey *leads to* getting drunk.
- *You always* get drunk from drinking a whole bottle of whiskey.
- Drinking a whole bottle of whiskey *can't help but make you* drunk.

Unfortunately, these expressions occur primarily in the parts of the argumentation that are often left unexpressed. Fortunately, the explicit argument, too, often holds clues that help identify the type of argumentation.

In argumentation based on a symptomatic relation, either the argument or the standpoint often contains a predicate noun that is further qualified with words like *real, born, typical* or *a prime example of*:

Louise can really hold people's interest, because she is a *born* teacher.

This is not a *real* report, because it doesn't even have a bibliography.

I'm already completely recovered, because I am a *typical* Leo.

Argumentation based on analogy can often be recognized by words like *also, either,* or *any more than* in the explicit argument, and *the same* or *just like* in the standpoint:

It would be ridiculous if the telephone company made you pay for dialing a number that wasn't answered. I mean, you don't have to pay for a ticket to the movies if they're already sold out *either*.

You should hire the *same* band as Eric had for his party, because it was a great success.

Argumentation based on a causal relation can often be recognized by words that predict that a certain consequence will ensue, such as *then, otherwise, because of that* or *that leads to*. If such words appear in the argumentation, they often also signal pragmatic argumentation, as in the second and third examples below:

> The sale of valuable works of art to anonymous buyers will make it difficult for museums to borrow art from private collections, because *then* you won't be able to trace the owners.
>
> Of course authors want to be paid well. *Otherwise* they wouldn't be able to make a living from their writing.
>
> We can't make public what is really going on, because *it would lead to* embarrassment of certain highly placed party members.

Other clues that argumentation is of the causal type are verbs and expressions that refer to the origin or consequence of something, such as *create, make, arise from* or *catch*:

> You shouldn't keep on pouting, because it *makes* me feel guilty.
>
> Fred may very well have *caught* a cold, because he has constantly been sitting in drafts.

FURTHER READING

An overview of the state of the art in the various approaches to the study of argument schemes is provided in "Argument schemes" by B. J. Garssen in F. H. van Eemeren (Ed.), *Crucial Concepts in Argumentation Theory*, Amsterdam: Amsterdam University Press, 2001, chapter 4. F. H. van Eemeren and R. Grootendorst provide in *Argumentation, Communication, and Fallacies*, Hillsdale, NJ: Lawrence Erlbaum Associates, 1992, chapter 9, a pragma-dialectical account of argument schemes. A somewhat different approach is advocated by D. N. Walton in *Argumentation Schemes for Presumptive Reasoning*, Mahwah, NJ: Lawrence Erlbaum Associates, 1996. In M. Leff, "Commonplaces and argumentation in Cicero and Quintilian," *Argumentation*, 1996, vol. 10, no. 2, pp. 445–454, some aspects of the classical approach to argument schemes are discussed. See D. Ehninger and W. Brockriede, *Decision by Debate*, New York/London: Harper & Row (2nd ed.), 1978, for a classification of sorts of argumentation inspired by the Toulmin model of argumentation.

EXERCISES

1. Does the following text contain an inconsistency? If so, what is the nature of this inconsistency?

   a. *Re: media causing violence in kids*

      This is another case of society looking for a scapegoat. When books came out, people thought they were horrible things with all sorts of evil intent. The same with rock and roll, TV, and now video games share the blame.

      I have been killing everything from space invaders to mutant spiders to delta force guys since the days of Atari, and I have not yet picked up a weapon and murdered real people once. The thought never occurs to me.

      The only reason why kids display this behavior is because the parents won't take responsibility for them. These parents don't want to take the time to raise their kids, they expect the TV to do it, and then blame the TV when their kids go bad.

      Face it, TV and video games are for adults now, not children. If parents don't mind their children watching horrific shows and playing violent video games, that's fine. But the parents have to show the kid what is real and what is not.

2. Is the observation of an inconsistency in the following text correct and if so, what is the nature of the inconsistency?

   b. *Dog and gun*

      The Labour Member of Parliament Kate Hoey writes (March 6): "A ban on hunting with dogs is not the answer. It is unenforceable, it is an attack on a freedom long cherished by citizens, it will destroy jobs and, crucially, it will do nothing for animal welfare."

      Coming from a party that prohibited target shooting with pistols, this is most surprising. If I may paraphrase ... "A ban on target shooting with pistols is not the answer. Its unenforceable, it is an attack on a freedom long cherished by citizens, it will destroy jobs and, crucially it will do nothing for public safety."

      Consistency please, Ms. Hoey.

3. Which type of argumentation is used in the following examples?

   a. Six of the race-horses stolen in Devon (England) have been found in Sweden. Because they were the best horses in Sir Edgar's stables, the police think the thieves must be experts.

b. He could easily do without freedom, since he is always sitting in his room anyhow.

c. Those short film fragments are confusing. Just when you start to get some idea what it's all about, another theme is introduced.

d. They probably bought their furniture on credit, because when going through their belongings we came across a mail-order catalog.

e. *Interviewer:*

   You say you are not superstitious? So you don't read your horoscope or anything like that?
   Ian Hart:

   I do if I'm bored and I've read the paper from cover to cover. But I also read the advertisements for incontinence undergarments—doesn't mean I believe in them.

f. *From "The murder of captain Joseph White," a speech from Daniel Webster (1782–1852):*

   Let me ask your attention, in the first place, to those appearances, on the morning after the murder, which have a tendency to show that it was done in pursuance of a preconcerted plan of operation. What are they? A man was found murdered in his bed. No stranger had done the deed, no one unacquainted with the house had done it. It was apparent that somebody from within had opened, and that somebody from without had entered. There had obviously and certainly been concert and cooperation. The inmates of the house were not alarmed when the murder was perpetrated. The assassin had entered without any riot or any violence. He had found the way prepared before him. The house had been previously opened. The window was unbarred from within, and its fastening unscrewed. There was a lock on the door of the chamber in which Mr. White slept, but the key was gone. It had been taken away and secreted. The footsteps of the murderer were visible, outdoors tending toward the window. The plank by which he entered the window still remained. The road he pursued had been thus prepared for him. The victim was slain, and the murderer had escaped. Everything indicated that somebody from within had cooperated with somebody from without. Everything proclaimed that some of the inmates, or somebody having access to the house, had had a hand in the murder.

On the face of the circumstances, it was apparent, therefore, that this was a premeditated, concerted murder; that there had been a conspiracy to commit it.

g. In South America drugs will remain a more important export product than coffee and sugar, since the West is willing to pay a fair price for cocaine and not for coffee and sugar.

h. *No conspiracy, Mr. Fayed*

The Sunday Times today publishes the personal testimony of Britain's most controversial figure, Mohammed al-Fayed. In this he takes issue with the official account of the death of Diana, Princess of Wales. The owner of Harrods, the London store and the father of the princess's lost love, Dodi al-Fayed, clearly believes that he and his family are the victims of an Establishment plot that embraces the political classes, the security forces and the media.

We sympathize with him for his loss but we do not believe his conspiracy to be true. The deaths of glamorous figures have always provoked conspiracy theories. President John Kennedy's assassination and Marilyn Monroe's death were followed by outrageous allegations. Once the evidence was made public, however, a fair-minded examination robbed the conspiracy theories of credibility. Most people now have little difficulty believing Kennedy was assassinated by a lone gunman, Lee Harvey Oswald, and that Monroe died of a drug overdose.

i. *Lincoln to those who urged a change of commanders in the middle of the Civil War:*

"Gentlemen, I want you to suppose a case for a moment. Suppose that all the property you were worth was in gold, and you had put it in the hands of Blondin, the famous ropewalker, to carry across the Niagara Falls on a tight rope. Would you shake the rope while he was passing over it, or keep shouting to him, 'Blondin, stoop a little more! Go a little faster!' No, I am sure you would not. You would hold your breath as well as your tongue, and keep your hands off until he was safely over. Now, the government is in the same situation. It is carrying an immense weight across a stormy ocean. Untold treasures are in its hands. It is doing the best it can. Don't badger it! Just keep still, and it will get you safely over."

4. On what kind of argument does Calvin base his (implicit) standpoint that the tooth fairy cannot be very bright?

7
Fallacies (1)

W hen evaluating argumentative discourse, fallacies in the discourse must be detected. Fallacies are violations of the rules for critical discussion that prevent or hinder the resolution of a difference of opinion. They can occur during any of the discussion stages and can be committed by either party. In the presentation of standpoints and arguments, the following moves are among the fallacies that may threaten the resolution process: (1) putting the opponent under pressure or attacking him personally (violation of freedom rule), (2) evading or shifting the burden of proof (violation of burden-of-proof rule), (3) setting up a straw man (violation of standpoint rule), (4) using irrelevant argumentation or rhetorical tricks (violation of relevance rule), and (5) denying or magnifying an unexpressed premise (violation of unexpressed premise rule).

7.1 VIOLATIONS OF THE FREEDOM RULE

There are a variety of ways in which parties to a difference of opinion can make resolution difficult or even impossible. This can happen during any stage of the discussion. Parties do not always do this on purpose. But each way of impeding the progress of the discussion constitutes a violation of the discussion rules that must be followed in order to successfully resolve a difference of opinion. Such violations of the discussion rules are known as *fallacies*.

Violations are often difficult to spot. That is what is so treacherous about fallacies. Strictly speaking, there can be a fallacy in discourse only if the discourse is argumentative in nature, that is, if it is an attempt to resolve a difference of opinion. But not every discussion is argumentative; a discussion may be purely informative or be intended to entertain. In case of doubt, it is advisable to treat a discourse as an argumentative discussion and assume that both parties are willing to work toward a resolution of their difference of opinion and will follow the rules for doing this.

There are 10 rules that apply specifically to argumentative discussions. The first 5 rules pertain to how parties should put forward their standpoints and arguments in order to work constructively toward a resolution of the difference of opinion. These rules are discussed in this chapter. The other 5 rules pertain to the argumentation and the conclusion of the discussion. These rules are discussed in chapter 8. Although observing these 10 rules does not guarantee that the difference of opinion will be satisfactorily resolved, violating them will surely prevent such a resolution. Fallacies can be identified by referring to these rules.

Rule 1: Parties Must Not Prevent Each Other From Putting Forward Standpoints or Casting Doubt on Standpoints

A difference of opinion can be satisfactorily resolved only if it is first brought to light. To avoid interfering with this process, parties to a discussion must give each other unlimited freedom to put forward and to criticize standpoints and arguments. This requirement is stated in Rule 1.

Violations of Rule 1 sometimes occur during the confrontation stage. The result is that the difference of opinion does not come to light, or not completely, and therefore has no chance of being resolved. Rule 1 can be violated in two ways: by placing limits on the standpoints or doubts that may be expressed, or by restricting a party's freedom of action.

One way to limit the expression of standpoints and doubts is to declare certain standpoints sacrosanct, or not open to question:

I'm going to have the kitchen remodeled. We can discuss style and layout or anything you want, but not whether it will be done.

Another way of imposing limitations is to declare certain standpoints taboo:

I don't think you should say that Grandmother shouldn't have remarried. One should not speak ill of the dead.

Restricting the other party's freedom of action is an attempt to dismiss him as a serious party to the discussion. Two ways of doing this are (a) to put him under pressure not to put forward a certain standpoint or objection or (b) to discredit him in the eyes of the public by casting doubt on his expertise, integrity, or credibility.

There are many ways to prevent a standpoint or an objection from being presented. The most effective of these is, of course, to keep the opponent out of the discussion by using physical force. Simply the threat of violence or other sanctions may also be quite effective.

Any threat that aims to restrict the other party from freely putting forward his standpoint or criticism is called a *fallacy of the stick* (*argumentum ad baculum*). Sometimes the threat is expressed very directly: "If you try to get the city council to approve that, I will send my thugs after you." Usually it is done in a more subtle way. Indirect reference may be made to unpleasant consequences for the other party if the speaker does not get his way: "Of course you must make your own decision, but remember that we're one of your top clients." Or the speaker may emphatically deny any intention of putting on pressure: "I certainly wouldn't want you to be influenced by the fact that I happen to be chair of the committee that will be evaluating your work."

Another effective way of putting pressure on the other party is to play on his emotions: "How can you have given me a failing mark for my thesis? I've worked on it night and day." Such a fallacious move is called an *appeal to pity* (*argumentum ad misericordiam*).

In addition to threats, emotional blackmail, and other ways of restricting the other party's moves, there are also ways to discredit him. Presenting the other party to listeners as stupid, unreliable, biased, or otherwise unworthy of credibility is a way to make sure his arguments will fall on deaf ears. It in effect denies him the right to participate in the discussion by convincing the audience that there is no use listening to him. In principle, personal characteristics of the other party should not be brought into the discussion unless they play a direct role in it, for example because the reliability of a witness is under question.

A personal attack is characterized by being directed not at the intrinsic merits of someone's standpoint or doubt, but at the person itself. The traditional Latin name for this fallacy is *argumentum ad hominem*. There are various kinds of personal attacks. One type is a *direct personal attack* on the other party, which, because of its insulting nature, is called the *abusive variant:*

> It made me so drowsy to read his response in last week's edition that I will not even take the trouble to reply to his musings. The man is weak in the head, and blessed are the innocent of spirit.

In a direct personal attack, what is being kicked is the person rather than the ball. The impression is given that someone stupid or evil could not possibly have a correct standpoint or a reasonable doubt. Attackers hope in this way to be relieved of the obligation to give reasons for their criticism of the other party's position.

In the second type, suspicion is cast on the other party's motives, for example by suggesting that the party has a personal interest in the matter and is therefore biased. This is an *indirect personal attack* that is known as the *circumstantial variant*. The following passage from a letter to the editor contains such an indirect personal attack:

> Marilyn French believes that men are the cause of the disadvantaged position of women and of environmental problems. I cannot avoid the impression that French must at some time in the past have washed the dirty socks of a man she did not love much, and therefore stopped thinking.

In an indirect personal attack, someone's opinion is claimed to derive from suspect personal motives, and the arguments advanced are unmasked as rationalizations.

In the third type of an *argumentum ad hominem*, an attempt is made to undermine the other party's credibility by pointing out a contradiction in that party's words or deeds, for example a contradiction between their opinions in the past and the present, or between what they say and what they do. This type is called the *you also variant* (*tu quoque*): You also do or think differently from what could reasonably be expected. The following letter to the editor argues that there is a contradiction between Mrs. Gardner's opinions on the AFP test and her own behavior:

> Mrs. A. Gardner discourages people from participating in the so-called AFP test, which measures the chances of a pregnant woman having a baby with *spina bifida* or Down's syndrome. Mrs. Gardner knows all about the consequences of the AFP test. So why did she have such an AFP test done herself? Because in fact she preferred not to have a mongoloid baby?

The reasoning behind the you also variant is that anyone who is not consistent cannot be right. Anyone who does not practice what he or she preaches is, of course, being inconsistent. But this does not automatically mean that their standpoint is wrong. To be able to establish the acceptability of the standpoint, the arguments must first be evaluated.

Note that pointing out inconsistencies is a fallacy only if it is based on inconsistency with a standpoint that the opponent has advanced outside the discussion. If someone puts forward contradictory standpoints or arguments in the course of the discussion, then it is not a fallacy to point this out. On the contrary, identifying inconsistencies in the discussion itself is a necessary part of the evaluation.

7.2   VIOLATIONS OF THE BURDEN-OF-PROOF RULE

Rule 2: A Party Who Puts Forward a Standpoint Is Obliged to Defend It if Asked to Do So

To resolve a difference of opinion, a person who puts forward a standpoint must be prepared to defend this standpoint, and a person who calls a standpoint into question must be prepared to assume the role of antagonist. This latter requirement seldom poses a problem because someone who voluntarily criticizes a standpoint can hardly object to taking on the role of antagonist. However, not everyone who expresses a standpoint is eager to actually defend it.

Protagonists can be released from the obligation to defend their standpoint if they have previously defended it successfully against the same antagonist and if nothing has changed in either the starting points or the discussion rules. In this case, the defense would be a pointless repetition. Protagonists can also be released from the obligation to defend their standpoint if their opponents refuse to commit themselves to anything and are not prepared to follow the rules. In such a situation, it would be pointless to defend the standpoint because the necessary conditions for resolving the disagreement are not met.

Rule 2 is violated when someone tries to get out of the obligation to defend a standpoint. If they get away with it, the discussion will stagnate in the opening stage, in which it is determined who is protagonist and who is antagonist.

The most drastic way to escape the obligation to defend your standpoint is to shift the burden of proof onto the person criticizing the standpoint: "You first prove that it isn't so." This is committing the fallacy of *shifting the burden of proof*.

In a nonmixed difference of opinion, only one party puts forward a standpoint, so there is only one party who has anything to defend. In this case, shifting the burden of proof is entirely unjustified because someone who criticizes a standpoint does not bear any burden of proof. The antagonist is then being saddled with the role of protagonist of the opposite standpoint, even though the antagonist has not advanced a standpoint at all. The following text gives a good example of the use of this trick in Holland, where viewers are obliged to pay TV tax:

> The Minister of Cultural Affairs mentions "the successful hunt for TV tax evaders." That is a good example of a fallacy. The hunt goes like this: on March 11 you receive a letter from the TV tax office that announces "A different look at your favorite program." You read that your name and address are not in "our database" and since "these days nearly every home has a television," you are asked to pay your TV tax. Let us assume that you are one of the few persons who have no time to watch TV or no interest in what TV has to offer. You have no TV in your home. You would like to just throw away the unpleasant letter, but you can't just do that. There is a form that you have to fill out stating that you have no TV. What the Minister of Cultural Affairs calls a "successful hunt" is a plain and simple shifting of the burden of proof.

In a mixed difference of opinion, the situation is more complicated. Because both parties have advanced a standpoint, they each have an obligation to defend their own standpoint. The only decision to be made is in what order they should present their defenses.

This problem of deciding the order of defense is often incorrectly seen as a problem of choice. One party often attempts to lay the burden of proof at the door of the other party, usually the one who is attacking received wisdom, established opinion, traditional views, or the existing state of affairs. The burden of proof then rests with the party who wants to change the status quo; he or she must prove that the proposed alternative is better. In the terminology of criminal law, one can say that the status quo has the status of *presumption*. In the following text this principle of presumption is appealed to:

> Supporters of the change are demanding that opponents show that reducing working hours would have undesirable consequences, such as reduced demand for labor or stagnation of the economy. But in fact, it is customary that supporters of a far-reaching measure (and reducing working hours is indeed far-reaching) must show that such a measure will have a beneficial effect, rather than that the other side must show that it may have harmful consequences.

Applying the principle of presumption, however, must not result in the burden of proof in a mixed dispute being assigned unilaterally to one of the parties.

Another criterion that can help decide the order in which standpoints are to be defended in mixed disputes is a principle known in civil law as the principle of *fairness*. According to this principle, the standpoint that is easiest to defend should be defended first. A legal expert, Mr. Maarten Henket, once gave a good example of apportioning the burden of proof according to the principle of fairness:

> An example of an exception to the rule "He who makes a claim must prove it" can be found in alimony cases. Let us take the familiar situation of a woman who has a right to alimony from her ex-husband. The woman notices that her ex-husband's income has gone up and wants more alimony. According to the rule just stated, she should have to prove that his income has risen. That is very difficult, in view of bank privacy and so on, and in practice the judge shifts the burden of proof to the husband: he must put his papers on the table and then it will be seen whether his income has gone up or not. This conflicts with the rule "He who makes a claim must prove it."

The principle of presumption and the principle of fairness may help in certain situations when deciding what order to follow, but a mixed difference of opinion can never be completely resolved in an argumentative discussion unless both of the parties meet the obligation to defend their standpoints. A subtle way to avoid the obligation to defend a standpoint is to present the standpoint as something that needs no proof at all. The protagonist in this case is guilty of committing the fallacy of *evading the burden of proof*. A person commits this fallacy when presenting the standpoint as something that is self-evident: "It is obvious that ...," "Nobody in their right mind would deny that ...," "It goes without saying that ...." If this ploy works, antagonists may feel overwhelmed and fail to voice their doubts.

The protagonist can sometimes achieve a similar effect by giving a personal guarantee for the correctness of the standpoint: "I can assure you that ...," "There is no doubt in my mind that ...," "I am absolutely convinced that ...," "You can take it from me that ...."

Another ploy for evading the burden of proof is to formulate the standpoint in a way that amounts to *making it immune to criticism* because it cannot be tested or evaluated. Examples of such *hermetic* formulations of standpoints are "Women are by nature possessive," "Men are basically hunters," "The Frenchman is essentially intolerant," and "The youth of today are lazy." These standpoints refer to "men," "women," "the youth," "the Frenchman," avoiding quantifiers such as "all," "some," "most," or "the average." Often, intangible (*essentialistic*) qualifications, such as "essentially," "real," "by nature," are used as well. Because of the imprecise formulation, it is unclear how the standpoint in question can be satisfactorily defended or refuted. How many examples or counterexamples are needed? If an attempt is made to refute the standpoint "Women are by nature possessive" by citing one or more examples of women who are not possessive, the opponent will most likely claim that these counterexamples are irrelevant because the women cited in these examples are not "real" women or are not acting according to their "true nature." All attempts at refutation thus bounce off an armor of immunity.

7.3   VIOLATIONS OF THE STANDPOINT RULE

Rule 3: A Party's Attack on a Standpoint Must Relate to the Standpoint That Has Indeed Been Advanced by the Other Party

Rule 3 is violated when the standpoint attacked is not the standpoint that was originally put forward by the protagonist. This causes a shift in the proposition with respect to which one party adopts a positive and the other party a neutral standpoint, so that in effect, and often without it being noticed, the difference of opinion becomes multiple. If parties talk at cross purposes like this, it will be impossible for them to resolve the original disagreement. Even if the disagreement seems to be resolved, it will be, at most, a spurious resolution. What the one party seems to have successfully defended is not the same as what the other party has attacked.

Such shifts in standpoint can occur during any stage of the discussion. It may happen at the very beginning of the discussion, in the confrontation stage, if the antagonist's criticism turns out to be directed at a different standpoint than the one the protagonist has advanced. During the opening stage, the parties may be referring to a different proposition than the one that formed the starting point of the discussion in the confrontation stage. During the argumentation stage, it may be that the arguments of the protagonist and the antagonist relate to two different propositions. In addition, the conclusion of the discussion may be worded in such a way that it, in fact, relates to a proposition somewhat different from the one in the original dispute.

There are two different ways of attacking a standpoint that is not really the one presented by the opponent. The original standpoint can be misrepresented, or a fictitious standpoint can be attributed to the opponent. In either case, the strategy is more likely to succeed with an audience that does not know exactly what the opponent's original standpoint was.

Parties who misrepresent the opponent's standpoint or attribute a fictitious standpoint to him or her commit the fallacy of the *straw man*. In both cases, they plan their attack by taking the path of least resistance: They attribute to their opponent a standpoint that can be attacked more easily. By distorting their opponent's standpoint, they set up a straw man that they can easily knock down. In the most extreme case, the standpoint attacked does not show any resemblance to the original standpoint, but sometimes the two standpoints differ only in details.

One of the techniques for attributing a fictitious standpoint to the other party is to emphatically put forward the opposite standpoint. If someone says firmly, "I personally believe the defense of our democracy is of great importance," she thereby suggests that her opponent thinks otherwise. If the opponent does not hasten to declare that he too is a great champion of democracy, he immediately draws on himself the suspicion that he does not support democracy.

Another way of attributing a fictitious standpoint to the opponent is to refer to a group to which the opponent belongs and to link that group with the fictitious standpoint:

> She says that she thinks this research is useful, but as a business person she naturally sees it as a waste of money.

Here the speaker implies that it is obvious what this group (business people) thinks about this matter and that what applies to the group applies to all individual members of the group.

In a third technique, not only the standpoint is fictitious, but the opponent too. By using expressions such as "Nearly everyone thinks that ...," "Educators are of the opinion that ...," and "Everyone has been saying lately that ...," it is not stated who actually holds the standpoint being attacked. There is no reference made to surveys, opinion polls, or other evidence that there really are people who adhere to the standpoint.

When the opponent's standpoint is misrepresented, it is presented in a way that makes it more difficult to defend, or even untenable or ridiculous. This is often achieved by taking a standpoint out of context, by oversimplifying it, or by exaggerating it, as in the following complaint:

> The result is very discouraging because of the way he goes about things: quoting some sentences completely out of context, suggesting meanings that aren't there, and finally, with several well-chosen exaggerations—which aren't there either—making the prey ripe for his omniscient and omnivorous voracity. I find this a superficial way of discussing academic work.

Exaggerating a standpoint by generalizing it may be accomplished by leaving out quantifiers like "some" and "a few" and replacing them with "all." The resulting standpoint is much easier to attack. If you are defending the standpoint that some men are oversensitive, your job is done as soon as you have given a couple of examples of oversensitive men. Defending the standpoint that "all" men are oversensitive is naturally much more difficult; your opponent has only to give one example of an insensitive man to show that your standpoint is untenable.

Techniques often used in simplifying standpoints are to leave out nuances and restrictions. A good example of the first is accusing someone of having written that homeopaths are charlatans, whereas what the person had actually written was that homeopaths are a group "in which the line between legitimate and charlatan is very fuzzy."

If the original formulation of the disputed standpoint can be consulted, it is possible to verify whether it has been represented accurately. This is difficult if the original formulation is not available. Sometimes, however, the representation is so improbable that it is immediately suspect. An example of such a suspect representation of a standpoint occurs in a Senator's response to a Deputy Health Secretary's argumentation for his plans to promote sports as leisure-time pursuits:

> The first argument, whose unsoundness is obvious, has to do with the costs of health care. The Deputy Secretary is afraid that parts of the body that are little used will quickly become brittle or fall off, after which the help of the medical establishment—charging for a single day what an average person earns in a month—will be needed. Since sports trainers are cheaper than surgeons, health care costs can be reduced if more people participate in sports.

In other cases, it helps to watch out for certain signals in the way the standpoint is represented. Some skepticism is called for when the speaker too emphatically proclaims the opponent's standpoint: "Clearly the author is of the opinion that ...," "The author obviously assumes that ..." Although the formulations suggest otherwise, it often turns out that the standpoint proclaimed was not the author's standpoint.

7.4   VIOLATIONS OF THE RELEVANCE RULE

Rule 4: A Party May Defend His or Her Standpoint Only by Advancing Argumentation Related to That Standpoint

Rule 4 places two minimum requirements on the defense of standpoints: The defense must be conducted by means of arguments, and those arguments must be genuinely relevant to the standpoint being defended. If the antagonist fails to notice that these requirements have not been met, he or she may end up accepting the standpoint on the basis of an irrelevant argument. In this case, the difference of opinion has not really been resolved.

Violations of Rule 4 occur during the argumentation stage. There are two kinds of violations. The first is when the argumentation has no relation whatsoever to the standpoint that was advanced in the confrontation stage. This is a case of *irrelevant argumentation*. The second kind of violation is when a standpoint is defended with means other than argumentation, while at the same time the protagonist acts as though he or she were providing argumentation. This is called *non-argumentation*.

Irrelevant argumentation, in fact, defends a standpoint that is not the standpoint that caused the difference of opinion. Just as in the case of the straw man, there is a shift in the proposition to which the standpoint relates. But in the case of irrelevant argumentation, it is the protagonist who distorts his or her own standpoint. Instead of making it easier to attack, the shift is intended to make the standpoint easier to defend. Then the fallacy is committed of putting forward *argumentation relevant only to a standpoint that is not the one at issue*, which is better known as *ignoratio elenchi*. Here is an example:

> Amateur sports are being ruined by all the alcohol that is sold at sports canteens, because research shows that 85% of all sports canteens sell alcohol.

At first sight the argument and the standpoint seem to be related, but actually the argument (alcohol is sold in 85% of all sports canteens) does not support the standpoint that "amateur sports are being ruined by all the alcohol that is sold at sports canteens." The argument would, however, support a different standpoint: "It is easy to buy alcohol in sports canteens."

When non-argumentation is used, it is not usually for the purpose of convincing the other party, but of winning over a third party. Instead of putting forward argumentation to support the standpoint at issue, the protagonist plays on the emotions, sentiments or biases of the intended audience. If we use the classical categories of means of persuasion—*logos, ethos,* and *pathos*—we could say that *pathos* takes the place of *logos* here. That is why playing on the emotions of the audience is called a *pathetic fallacy.*

Pathetic fallacies generally thrive in public discussions about which many people have strong feelings. In such situations, whoever most successfully manipulates the (positive or negative) feelings of the audience has the best chance of having a standpoint accepted. Examples of positive emotions that can be appealed to are feelings of security or loyalty. Examples of negative emotions that can be appealed to are fear, greed, and shame. The following letter to the editor accuses one of the participants in a discussion on anti-terrorism of playing on people's sentiments:

> When Mr. Carter talks about innocent women and children who have been victims of terrorism, he is playing unfairly on the sentiments of the members of the jury. Because in fact it is just as terrible a thing when the victims are men, whether they are ordinary men, police agents, or soldiers.

Appeals to prejudices and emotions are not normally presented as if they were arguments. It often suffices to emphasize in an emotional way the significance of certain interests or values. The audience itself will make the desired connection between these and the standpoint at issue.

In addition to the rhetorical means of persuasion *pathos*, a protagonist may also make use of *ethos*. Aristotle believed this means to be the most effective. Speakers use *ethos* when they attempt to decide the difference of opinion in their favor on the strength of their own expertise or good character. They attempt to increase the audience's faith in their expertise, credibility, or integrity, so that the audience will simply take their word for the standpoint's acceptability. If a protagonist has a particularly strong *ethos*, he or she may not need to present any defense at all for the standpoint.

In itself, there is nothing wrong with making use of *ethos*. In many cases, there is no other choice than to accept something on the authority of experts. Certain topics require so much specialized knowledge that laypeople cannot independently verify them. In other instances, the protagonist may be the only witness to a certain event or the only one who can verify the accuracy of a certain statement. Examples of this are statements about the speaker's own mood or physical well-being. There is nothing wrong with depending on someone else's judgment in such cases, but it is important to realize that a difference of opinion cannot really be resolved in this way because it is left to the expert to settle the dispute.

Something to watch out for, however, is when a person who claims to have expertise does not actually possess it or when the expertise is not relevant to the matter at hand. Then the *ethical fallacy* of *abuse of authority* is committed (which is on a par with the fallacy that is traditionally known as *argumentum ad verecundiam*). An example of this is when someone suggests, without providing actual argumentation, that he or she possesses the required amount of expertise on the basis of being a professor and proceeds to make statements about the dangers of nuclear energy, when in fact his field of expertise is Egyptology.

7.5 VIOLATIONS OF THE UNEXPRESSED PREMISE RULE

Rule 5: A Party May Not Falsely Present Something as a Premise That Has Been Left Unexpressed by the Other Party or Deny a Premise That He or She Has Left Implicit

Violations of Rule 5 are related to the fact that in everyday language, all kinds of things are implied or are expressed only indirectly.

Parties to a discussion of course should not try to take improper advantage of implicit or indirect language. That is what happens when the antagonist attacks the protagonist by producing a reconstruction of the unexpressed premise that goes further than what the protagonist can actually be held to. Exaggerating the unexpressed premise makes the standpoint easier to attack, and the fallacy is called *magnifying what has been left unexpressed*. Protagonists can violate Rule 5 by refusing to accept commitment to an unexpressed premise implied by their own defense, thereby committing the fallacy of *denying an unexpressed premise*.

Violations of Rule 5 occur during the argumentation stage. The result is that the difference of opinion cannot be brought to resolution because parties deny their commitments or put words in each other's mouth. Rule 5 essentially means that protagonists can be held to nothing they are not really committed to and to everything they really are committed to.

The fallacy of magnifying an unexpressed premise consists of adding an unexpressed premise that goes beyond what is warranted and attributing a premise to the protagonist that goes beyond the commitments created by the protagonist's defense. In the following example, Heather commits this fallacy:

> Jerome: It could be that he doesn't like dogs very much, because he has a cat.
>
> Heather: So you think that everyone who has a cat by definition hates dogs?
>
> Jerome: No, I didn't say that. I only mean that there are a lot of cat owners who don't much like dogs.

Given the cautious way Jerome has formulated his standpoint ("It could be ..."), it is incorrect to attribute to him the unexpressed premise that *everyone* who has a cat *by definition* hates dogs. Furthermore, "not liking dogs much" is not the same as "hating dogs." In this respect as well, Heather has exaggerated what Jerome left unexpressed.

Speakers commit the fallacy of denying an unexpressed premise if they refuse responsibility for elements that are indeed implied by their defense. If the opponent correctly makes explicit something that is implied by the protagonist's argumentation, then the protagonist commits a fallacy by denying it. By hiding behind the claim "I never said that," the protagonist stands in the way of true resolution of the disagreement.

The inclination to deny unexpressed premises is strongest when they contain weak or controversial elements. The following is a good example:

> I have nothing against homosexuals. I just think that the age of consent for homosexual sex should not be lowered, because of the danger that young boys would be pushed into becoming homosexuals.

The use of the word "danger" is clear evidence that the speaker does not really have the tolerant attitude claimed in the first sentence: The unexpressed premise in this argumentation is that homosexuality is something that should be prevented if at all possible.

FURTHER READING

An influential historical study of fallacies is C. L. Hamblin, *Fallacies*, London: Methuen, 1970, reprinted by Vale Press, Newport News, VA. A formally oriented approach to the fallacies is also taken in J. Woods and D. Walton, *The Logic of the Fallacies*, Toronto: McGraw-Hill: Ryerson, 1982. The pragma-dialectical approach to the fallacies is explained in F. H. van Eemeren and R. Grootendorst, *Argumentation, Communication, and Fallacies: A Pragma-Dialectical Perspective*, Hillsdale, NJ: Lawrence Erlbaum Associates, 1992, chapters 8–19. An overview of the state of the art in the study of the fallacies is provided by F. H. van Eemeren in F. H. van Eemeren (Ed.), *Crucial Concepts in Argumentation Theory*, Amsterdam: Amsterdam University Press, 2001, chapter 6.

EXERCISES

1. Which of the following statements lend themselves, due to the fact that they are not falsifiable, to evasion of the burden of proof?
   a. Americans are racists.
   b. Americans are essentially racists.
   c. People are bad.
   d. Cathy is bad.
   e. Cathy cheats the social services.
   f. Doctors cheat the social services.

2. Do the following passages contain a violation of a discussion rule? If so, which fallacy has occurred?
   a. Martin Woolacott advocates the use of force against Iraq on the pretext that "the alternative, if it is to let Saddam prevail, is worse." In fact Saddam Hussein and his regime are essential for the stability and unity of Iraq. Notwithstanding his demonization in the West, his military regime, to many Iraqis, remains synonymous with a united Iraq. If Saddam has done anything positive for his country, it has been to foster a sense of national pride and unity, which even the UN-led economic sanctions and U.S.-encouraged Kurds' rebellion in northern Iraq have failed to destroy. Should the West decide to remove Saddam by destroying his military and political structure, it should be ready to face the consequences: namely the possible break-up of Iraq. This would, in all probability, mean something like Lebanon of the 1980s or Somalia of the 1990s.
   b. *Letter to the editor:*
   I share Catherine Bennett's concern about Jeffrey Archer ending up as a serious candidate for Mayor of London, but not because of his fictional past, his questionable financial dealings, or even the quality of his writing—none of which disqualified other Tory politicians in the past 18 years. It is his politics that worry me.
   c. The project engineer says that Thompson is more qualified than I am to work on her project. But did you know that Thompson is engaged to her daughter?
   d. Capital punishment should be introduced in this country. You do want your children to live in a safe neighborhood, don't you?

e. To the Editor:
I take issue with your July 23 editorial "Hamptons Serenade," in which you describe the rich as shallow and undeserving.

I have a close friend who is a multimillionaire with a house in the Hamptons. We began in graduate school together in 1960. He dropped out of the Ph.D. program and went to work at an investment bank for $50 a week, while I got my Ph.D.

Now I make $75,000 a year, and he makes millions. Whenever I visit my friend, I feel nothing but pride in his accomplishment, and I feel good about knowing him.

I don't feel that wealth is "disorienting" or "strangely dislocating." I feel that I live in a great and free country—so free that a young guy like my friend who had no connections can end up a great success.

3. The following argument was given by a trade union against setting up a union for prostitutes in the Netherlands: "*We are opposed to prostitution because it exploits women and we cannot, therefore, regard it as a profession.*" To which of the following interpretations of this argument can the union be held committed?
   a. The exploitation of women is wrong.
   b. Something in which exploitation is involved cannot be a profession.
   c. Exploitation is wrong.

4. Which variants of the *argumentum ad hominem* occur in the passage given below from a column by the Dutch writer Gerrit Komrij? If necessary, follow the strategy of maximally argumentative interpretation.

Why the outcry over apartheid is so vehement in the Netherlands, of all places, is something that continues to amaze me. After all, no other country is itself so held together by apartheid. With a high and mighty attitude, the Dutch condemn a system which in their own country is an obsession. The passion for parochialism rages through institutions; everyone tries frenetically to preserve, to consolidate and to give preference to their own territory. However, as soon as the same thing happens in a far-away country, then it is regarded as the height of contemptibility. The Dutch fume with rage about the evil-smelling activities of others, while passing one foul wind after the other in their own back yard.

5. Think of a response to the following statements in which the burden of proof is evaded or shifted, a direct or indirect personal attack is launched, or there is a *tu quoque* or an *ad baculum*.

    a. *Wife to husband:* "You don't know how to manage money."

    b. *Aunt to nephew who is studying psychology:* "I really do wonder whether it is true that everything is due to sex."

    c. *Child to parents:* "I am perfectly capable of looking after myself."

    d. *Antique dealer to customer:* "You deliberately dropped that vase."

6. Are discussion rules violated in the following excerpts? If so, which fallacy has been committed?

    a. Many people are hurt terribly by little things we call "social slights." It is a well-known psychological fact that the people who become offended the easiest have the lowest self-esteem.

    b. *Alice:* You shouldn't take books from my bookshelf without asking, and then lend them to someone else.
    Betty: I did not take books out of your bookshelf, let alone lend any of your books to anyone else.
    Alice: Well, the books aren't on the bookshelf. YOU tell ME where they are.

    c. It is a fact that ulcers are not the result of what we ate, but what's eating us.

    d. Asked what steps Russia would take if Ukraine and the Baltic states of Estonia, Latvia and Lithuania were invited to join NATO, Mr. Yeltsin said he hoped the West would be "realistic" enough not to do it. "In NATO expansion, there is a red line for Russia which should not be crossed. Otherwise European stability might not withstand the new tension," he said.

    e. *Letter to the editor:*
    May I make it clear that the quotations attributed to me in your article about Pope John Paul's document on the protection of the Catholic faith were off-the-cuff remarks. I gave them to your correspondent as general briefing. I explained that I could not comment on the document itself until I had read it. The quotations therefore do not represent either my own considered opinion on the matter or that of the paper I edit.

8

Fallacies (2)

A *mong the fallacies that may occur in the argumentation stage are (6) falsely treating a starting point as agreed on, or denying a commitment to something that was an agreed-on starting point (violation of starting point rule), (7) using an inappropriate argument scheme or using an argument scheme incorrectly (violation of argument scheme rule), and (8) using invalid reasoning (violation of validity rule). In the concluding stage of the discussion (9) unwarranted consequences may be attached to a successful defense or a failed defense (violation of closure rule). Finally (10), the resolution of a difference of opinion can be obstructed during any stage of the discussion by the use of unclear or ambiguous language (violation of usage rule).*

8.1 VIOLATIONS OF THE STARTING POINT RULE

To satisfactorily resolve a difference of opinion, the parties to a discussion must give each other the freedom to express the difference of opinion, must be prepared to accept the burden of proof for their standpoints by presenting argumentation in their defense, must not falsely attribute standpoints or arguments to the other party, and must not try to dissociate themselves from the standpoints or arguments to which they have committed themselves. Although it is a big step forward if all these rules are followed, it is not sufficient. The arguments advanced should also meet several requirements.

A difference of opinion is resolved in favor of the protagonist if he conclusively defends his standpoint; otherwise, it is resolved in favor of the antagonist. The defense can be regarded as conclusive only if the arguments of the defense are directly acceptable to the opponent because they form part of the common starting points, or if they are acceptable because they are based on valid reasoning and appropriate argument schemes. If the parties fail to observe the rules for the conclusive defense of standpoints, their argumentation will contain fallacies that make their defense unacceptable.

Rule 6: No Party May Falsely Present a Premise as an Accepted Starting Point, or Deny a Premise Representing an Accepted Starting Point

Just as it is pointless to have a discussion with someone who refuses to abide by any discussion rules, it also makes no sense to have a discussion with someone who will not commit himself to any starting points. In order to resolve a difference of opinion, both parties must have in common some minimum of facts, beliefs, norms, and value hierarchies. If they cannot agree on any of these, they will never succeed in convincing each other of the acceptability of any standpoint. Ultimately, the defense of a standpoint rests on some set of statements that are acceptable to both parties.

Explicit agreements about common starting points are rare. Parties normally operate on the assumption that they share certain starting points. The better the parties know each other, the more likely it is that their assumptions about common starting points are accurate. Then it will sometimes be unnecessary to come to an explicit agreement about starting points.

The protagonist and antagonist do not actually have to believe that the propositions serving as common starting points are all true or acceptable, but they must conduct the discussion as if they believed this. Sometimes a proposition is temporarily accepted as true only in order to test its acceptability or even to demonstrate that it is unacceptable because it has untenable consequences. This would not be possible if both parties had to really believe in the acceptability of all of the starting points.

Rule 6 is violated if a party *falsely presents a premise as belonging to the common starting points* or *denies a premise that does in fact belong to the starting points.*

The *antagonist* violates Rule 6 if he questions either a proposition that was agreed on as a common starting point or one that the protagonist, based on verifiable background information, may rightly assume the antagonist to be committed to. A proposition with the status of starting point may not be questioned in the discussion. Of course, the proposition can always be questioned later in a separate discussion. If all assumptions are open to question at the same time, there cannot be a meaningful discussion, and the difference of opinion will never be resolved. The same is true if an antagonist in the middle of the discussion suddenly starts questioning a previously agreed-on proposition for opportunistic reasons: "But did I ever say the earth is round?," "But what is wrong with incest anyway?"

The *protagonist* violates Rule 6 if he acts as though a certain proposition was accepted as a starting point when that is not the case. A familiar trick for preventing a proposition from being attacked is to formulate something controversial in such an inconspicuous way that it is not noticed. This can be done by presenting the controversial proposition as a presupposition (an assumption tacitly assumed by the speaker) of another statement; for example, instead of directly saying "Fred is addicted to gambling," saying something like "I can't understand why Fred doesn't do something about that gambling addiction." In the second formulation, Fred's addiction to gambling is assumed, thus falsely giving the impression that the addiction is an established fact.

The protagonist can make unfair use of presuppositions not only in making assertions but also in asking questions:

Who have you quarreled with today?

If it has not yet been established that any quarreling took place, then the formulation of this question is misleading because it creates the impression that it is a common starting point that there has been a quarrel. To go about it properly, the question would need to be split in two: "Have you quarreled with anyone today?" and "Who have you quarreled with?" Asking the question in its original form is an example of the fallacy of *many questions*.

Another way protagonists sometimes wrongly assume that a proposition belongs to the common starting points is when in defending their standpoints they use an argument that amounts to the same thing as the standpoint. Because the standpoint is precisely that which is being debated, they know very well that a statement that is identical to or synonymous with the standpoint cannot possibly belong to the common starting points. If they nevertheless act as though it does, they are committing the fallacy of *circular reasoning* (also called *begging the question* or *petitio principii*).

Here is a simple example of circular reasoning:

> Racial discrimination is a punishable offense because it's against the law.

The circularity is perhaps not immediately obvious, until one realizes that "a punishable offense" implies violating the law. Thus, the argument and the standpoint in this example are nearly identical. A less obvious example of circular reasoning was challenged by Rudy Kousbroek (1970):

> In a recent issue of *Tirade*, G. van het Reve berates someone who took recourse to W.F. Hermans's motto: "the human being is a chemical process just like any other." Van het Reve attacked the motto by saying "I have never had a letter from a chemical process." This is a classic case of using that which has not been proved as proof: assuming the motto is correct, then Van het Reve will regularly and exclusively receive letters from chemical processes. (p. 37)

8.2   VIOLATIONS OF THE ARGUMENT SCHEME RULE

Rule 7: A Standpoint May Not Be Regarded as Conclusively Defended if the Defense Does Not Take Place by Means of an Appropriate Argument Scheme That Is Correctly Applied

Even if all of the statements making up the argumentation are accepted by both parties, the defense cannot be considered successful if these statements do not adequately support the standpoint (or whatever part of the argumentation they were intended to support). Only if the protagonist uses an appropriate argument scheme for his defense and applies that scheme correctly can the defense be judged successful. If the protagonist *uses an inappropriate argument scheme* or *applies a scheme in an incorrect way*, then he or she violates Rule 7. Such violations occur during the argumentation stage.

Some argument schemes are rarely acknowledged to be sound. The odds are that the opponent will not accept these schemes, so that a violation of Rule 7 occurs. One such scheme (a variant of argumentation based on a symptomatic relation) is the *populist fallacy* (*argumentum ad populum*). In the populist fallacy, the opinion of some number of people is used in arguing for the acceptance of the standpoint: It is claimed the standpoint should be accepted because so many people agree with it. However, in the following example it is pointed out that this is not true:

> Hundreds of thousands of cheering readers, viewers, or listeners are no proof at all of the correctness of an idea, and it is pure demagoguery to use their opinion as an argument.

Another well-recognized unsound way of arguing is to appeal inappropriately to a causal relation. The mistake of *confusing facts with value judgments* is a fallacy that is traditionally known as the *argumentum ad consequentiam*. In support of a standpoint with a factual proposition, an argument is advanced that is normative because it points out undesirable effects of the standpoint: "It isn't true, because I don't want it to be true" or "It's true, because I want it to be true." An example of *ad consequentiam* is:

> It can't be raining, because that would mean we'd have to cancel our picnic.

Even if the argument scheme itself is appropriate, not all ways of applying it are correct. If an argument scheme is correctly applied, then all critical questions corresponding to this scheme can be satisfactorily answered. For example, in committing a *fallacy of abuse of authority* (*argumentum ad verecundiam*), a proposition is presented as acceptable because some person or written source that is inappropriately presented as an authority says that it is so. This is a wrong application of a particular kind of argumentation based on a symptomatic relation.

Another example of improper use of an argument scheme based on a symptomatic relation is the *fallacy of hasty generalization* (*secundum quid*). The fallacy here is generalizing on the evidence of too few observations:

> After having spent our 1991 vacation in Cuba, we went there again in 1992, which shows that it's a great place for tourists.

The fact that one tourist couple is prepared to visit Cuba twice in a row is no proof that it is a great place for tourists in general.

If the argumentation is based on a relation of analogy, then the analogy must be a sound one. The two things compared must really be comparable and there must be no special circumstances that invalidate the comparison. If these requirements are not met, then we have the *fallacy of false analogy*.

When establishing causal relations, using the third main category of argument schemes, the reasoning may also go astray. Sometimes a cause-and-effect relation is based on no more than the fact that the one thing preceded the other. This is the *fallacy of post hoc ergo propter hoc* ("after this, therefore, because of this"). A soccer coach commits this fallacy by suggesting that the rise in ticket sales was due to his taking on the job:

> I like the Milan team. I like the way they play, their courage, their drive to win. Since I came we have gone from 40 to 71 thousand season ticket holders. There must be a reason for that.

Another common way of using a causal argument scheme incorrectly has to do with pragmatic argumentation. The mistake here is to wrongly suggest that adopting a certain course of action will inevitably be going from bad to worse, when in fact there is no evidence that such an effect will occur. Because it has not been shown that the predicted negative consequences will really ensue, one of the critical questions appropriate to causal argumentation cannot be satisfactorily answered. This is the *fallacy of the slippery slope*. A slippery slope can be detected in Gerrit Komrij's sketch of the consequences of government support of activities designed to protect women (but not homosexuals) from sexual violence:

> Those who find sexual violence important only when it is aimed at a limited and arbitrary group like girls and women will end up, if their reasoning is carried to its logical conclusion, finding any form of violence acceptable as long as it is aimed at an enemy specially marked out for that purpose.

8.3   VIOLATIONS OF THE VALIDITY RULE

Rule 8: The Reasoning in the Argumentation Must Be Logically Valid or Must Be Capable of Being Made Valid by Making Explicit One or More Unexpressed Premises

Violations of Rule 8 have long been considered to be the most important of the fallacies. Nevertheless, invalid reasoning is certainly not the most important cause of failure to reach resolution of a difference of opinion—if for no other reason than that arguments in everyday language, which are so often incomplete, can easily be rendered valid by filling in one or more premises.

Rule 8 is violated only if the reasoning, after making explicit everything that was left unexpressed, is still invalid. Violations have to do with the logical form of the reasoning underlying the argument.

There are several forms of faulty reasoning that occur with some regularity during the argumentation stage. The two best-known ones are *affirming the consequent* and *denying the antecedent*; these are the invalid counterparts of the *modus ponens* and *modus tollens* types of reasoning. The mistake made in both of these forms of invalid reasoning is that a sufficient condition is treated as a necessary condition. Lines of reasoning that take the form of affirming the consequent or denying the antecedent have the following pattern:

> If you eat spoiled fish (*antecedent*) you get sick. (*consequent*)
> Anne is sick. (*affirmation of the consequent*)
>
> *Therefore:*   Anne has eaten spoiled fish.

> If you eat spoiled fish (*antecedent*) you get sick. (*consequent*)
> Anne hasn't eaten any spoiled fish. (*denial of the antecedent*)
>
> *Therefore:*   Anne is not sick.

It is easy to see that both lines of reasoning are invalid when one stops to think that Anne could have got sick due to causes other than eating spoiled fish.

Another violation of Rule 8 is incorrectly attributing a property of the whole to the component parts or vice versa. The first is called the *fallacy of division*, the second the *fallacy of composition*. These fallacies involve treating the whole as a simple sum of the separate parts and assuming every property of the whole also applies to each of the component parts. But in fact, what is true for the parts is not necessarily true for the whole. If a stew is composed of ingredients each of which by itself is delicious, this is no guarantee that the stew will also be delicious. The following comment from the manager of the school cafeteria seems overly optimistic:

> We use real butter, real cream, and fresh lettuce, so our meals are always delicious!

Another example of the composition fallacy is:

> The Catholic church is a church for poor people.
>
> *Therefore:*   The Catholic church is poor.

What exactly is wrong with this argumentation? In the first place, it does not take into consideration the fact that the term "poor" is a *relative* one: Standards of wealth are different for individuals than for churches. Whether the Catholic church is poor or not can only be established by comparing its wealth with that of other churches or similar institutions. In the second place, the impression is given that the wealth of the church is simply the sum of the income and property of individual members, whereas *other factors* are involved, for instance, what portion of their income members donate to the church.

An example of the division fallacy is:

> The Cabinet is indecisive.
>
> *Therefore:*   The Ministers are indecisive.

In this argumentation, it is wrongly assumed that if the Cabinet as a whole is indecisive, then all of the members of the Cabinet are necessarily also indecisive. In fact, it is entirely possible that each member individually is decisive, but that each Minister wants something different so that the Cabinet as a whole is unable to reach a decision.

8.4   VIOLATIONS OF THE CLOSURE RULE

Rule 9: A Failed Defense of a Standpoint Must Result in the Protagonist Retracting the Standpoint, and a Successful Defense of a Standpoint Must Result in the Antagonist Retracting His or Her Doubts

Resolution can still be obstructed even in the last stage of the resolution process, when the argumentation is completed and the discussion only needs to be brought to a close. The concluding stage of the discussion must establish whether the difference of opinion has been resolved and in whose favor. If the parties do not succeed in coming to agreement on this, the difference of opinion persists. If the protagonist is convinced that the standpoint has been conclusively defended, but the antagonist insists that this is not so, then the discussion ends in a stalemate.

If the protagonist and the antagonist agree on the outcome, then they must also accept the consequences. A protagonist who has not managed to successfully defend the standpoint must be prepared to give up this standpoint. Otherwise, the protagonist commits the *fallacy of refusing to retract a standpoint that has not been successfully defended*. If, on the contrary, the protagonist has succeeded, then the antagonist must be prepared to retract the criticism of the standpoint. Otherwise, the antagonist commits the *fallacy of refusing to retract criticism of a standpoint that has been successfully defended*. Here is an example:

> Well, if that's the case, then I can't think of any more objections. But I still don't agree with it.

Other violations of Rule 9 arise when inflated consequences are attached to the successful attack or defense. Successful protagonists are entitled to expect the other party to retract their doubts about the standpoint, but no more than that. Otherwise, these protagonists commit the *fallacy of concluding that a standpoint is true because it has been defended successfully*. If protagonists conclude that they have now proved that their standpoint is true, then they are going too far. The only thing they have shown is that their standpoint, based on the agreed-on starting points, can be successfully defended. This does not imply that the standpoint is necessarily true or acceptable in any broader sense. The acceptability of the starting points outside the context of the discussion, after all, has not been established. The protagonist and antagonist do not even need to believe in the truth or acceptability of their common starting points. Likewise, the failure of a defense does not warrant the conclusion that the standpoint has been shown to be false or that the opposite standpoint is true. An antagonist who makes this claim is guilty of the *fallacy of concluding that a standpoint is true because the opposite has not been successfully defended* (*argumentum ad ignorantiam*).

The first mistake made in this fallacy is to confuse the roles of protagonist and antagonist. In a nonmixed difference of opinion, only one of the parties is obliged to defend their position, namely, the protagonist. The antagonist has merely doubted the standpoint, so it is impossible for him or her to have successfully defended the opposite standpoint. Only in a mixed discussion are there two protagonists and two standpoints, so that both protagonists are obliged to defend their positions. But even then, one party's defense failure does not cancel the other party's burden of proof.

The second mistake is to assume that the standpoint adopted in relation to a proposition must always be either positive or negative. This ignores the possibility of a "middle course," that is, taking a neutral position with no standpoint. If protagonists fail in their defense of a standpoint, this certainly does not mean that they must immediately accept the opposite standpoint. Anyone who acts as though this is a necessary consequence is committing the fallacy of *argumentum ad ignorantiam*. In the following example, both mistakes are made:

> Mother: You must never hit children, because then they lose trust in society and ten years later they'll be hitting everybody.
>
> Father: It has not in any way been proved that hitting children leads to violence later. So a slap once in a while for a good reason can't do any harm.

8.5 VIOLATIONS OF THE USAGE RULE

Rule 10: Parties Must Not Use Any Formulations That Are Insufficiently Clear or Confusingly Ambiguous, and They Must Interpret the Formulations of the Other Party as Carefully and Accurately as Possible

Unclear or ambiguous language can have direct negative consequences for the resolution of a difference of opinion. Lack of clarity during the confrontation stage can lead to a spurious disagreement, where the formulations chosen suggest a difference of opinion that does not exist. Lack of clarity can also lead to spurious agreement: The parties think they have reached agreement, when in fact their agreement is based on their having given different definitions to the terms used in the standpoint.

Ambiguity and lack of clarity in violation of Rule 10 can occur during any stage of the discussion. Any time a party makes use of unclear or ambiguous language to improve his or her own position in the discussion, they are guilty of the *fallacy of unclarity* or of the *fallacy of ambiguity*.

These fallacies occur not only by themselves, but also—even often—in combination with violations of other discussion rules. Lack of clarity sometimes accompanies a fallacy and enhances its effect. An *argumentum ad baculum* or an *argumentum ad hominem* is often more effective if the threat or accusation is made indirectly. Sometimes lack of clarity is inherent to a fallacy, for instance, the fallacy of magnifying an unexpressed premise. The antagonist can magnify an unexpressed premise precisely because it was not explicitly stated.

Some kinds of unclarity have to do with the structure of larger pieces of text; this is called *structural unclarity at the textual level*, resulting from "illogical" order, lack of coherence, obscure structure, and so on. Goudsblom describes the effect of such lack of clarity (in *Folia*, October 17, 1981):

> In many discussions ... a capricious intermingling takes place of descriptive, interpretive, explanatory and evaluative elements that results in an elusive combination of "sense" and "nonsense" that can perhaps best be termed "unsense." [...] It is striking how many discussions about politics and morals— that is, about society—are conducted by the grace of unsense. The starting points, the terms, the conclusions, even the statement of the problem, together constitute a hopeless tangle of description, interpretation, explanation and value judgment. To take part in such a discussion is to poke about in a rhetorical hornet's nest. This realization renders us powerless and speechless.

Four main types of unclarity at sentence level can be distinguished: unclarity resulting from (1) implicitness, (2) indefiniteness, (3) unfamiliarity, and (4) vagueness. The best way of explaining these is to give examples. Suppose someone says "Charles is a kleptomaniac." The listener may ask for clarification in any of a number of ways:

1   Are you warning me or just informing me?
2   Charles? Charles who?
3   A kleptomaniac? What's that?
4   What do you mean, he's a kleptomaniac? Do you mean once upon a time he stole something, or do you mean he makes a habit of stealing things?

Question 1 indicates the unclarity was due to *implicitness*: The listener is not sure what the communicative function of the speech act is because the context and situation allow for more than one interpretation.

Question 2 indicates the unclarity was due to *indefiniteness*; it seeks clarification of the propositional content. The listener cannot determine who the speaker is referring to; the *reference* is unclear.

Question 3 also indicates unclarity in the propositional content, but this time it is the *predication* that is problematic: The listener does not understand exactly what the speaker is trying to say about Charles because he does not know the meaning of the word "kleptomaniac" and perhaps has not even heard of the illness it designates. So the unclarity here is due to *unfamiliarity* with the word or with the illness it refers to.

Question 4 is the listener's attempt to obtain a clearer idea of what the speaker means by "kleptomaniac," thereby reducing the *vagueness* of this term. Although the listener knows the meaning of the word, he or she does not yet know what criteria the speaker is using. How often must someone steal to earn the label of "kleptomaniac"?

Ambiguity has to do with the fact that words and phrases can have more than one meaning. For example, the sentence "That is Herman's portrait" can be interpreted in three different ways: (1) the portrait was painted by Herman, (2) the portrait is owned by Herman, and (3) Herman is the subject of the portrait.

Questions can be ambiguous as well. There are, for instance, at least five possible interpretations of the question "Who is Tony?":

1   Which of you three is Tony?
2   Who in this picture is Tony?
3   Who is the actor that plays Tony?
4   What can you tell me about Tony?
5   Why the hell should we listen to Tony?

Ambiguity includes ambiguity of reference, as in the following sentence, where it is not clear who *her* refers to, Carla or Sandra:

Carla gave Sandra the mail; it was her last day here.

The following text offers a good example of a different kind of improper use of ambiguity:

Although Mr. Wylie claimed he would be open about everything, he started out by lighting up a large cigar and promptly disappeared in a cloud of smoke.... Mr. Wylie is silent when he should be speaking as a liberal.... Mr. Wylie smokes, and where there is smoke, there is fire.

The expression "where there is smoke there is fire" is used here in two senses. It is used literally, in that "smoke" refers to the smoke from Wylie's cigar, and it is used figuratively: Because Wylie himself says nothing about them there must be some truth to all the rumors about him. This use of ambiguity serves to camouflage the fact that the standpoint "Wylie is not being open" is being supported by the irrelevant argument that he smokes cigars.

FURTHER READING

In-depth studies of the fallacies can be found in J. Woods and D. Walton, *Fallacies: Selected Papers 1972–1982*, Berlin: Foris/Walter de Gruyter, 1989, and H. V. Hansen in R. C. Pinto (Eds.), *Fallacies: Classical and Contemporary Readings*, University Park, PA: Pennsylvania State University Press, 1995. See also D. N. Walton, *Informal Fallacies: Towards a Theory of Argument Criticisms*, Amsterdam-Philadelphia: John Benjamins, 1987, and *A Pragmatic Theory of Fallacies*, Tuscaloosa: University of Alabama Press, 1995. A discussion of Walton's approach to fallacies can be found in C. W. Tindale, "Fallacies, blunder and dialogue shifts: Walton's contributions to the fallacy debate," *Argumentation*, 1997, vol. 11, no. 3, pp. 341–354. For a typology of arguments from authority, see J. Goodwin, "Forms of authority and the real *ad verecundiam*," *Argumentation*, vol. 12, no. 2, pp. 267–280.

EXERCISES

1. Are the following arguments valid?
   a. *Pascal, quoted in an imaginary interview:*
      If you believe in God and he exists, then you are all right. If you believe in God and he does not exist, you haven't lost anything. If you do not believe in God and he does indeed exist, then you go to hell. And if you do not believe in God and he does not exist, you again haven't lost anything. It is, therefore, always better to believe in God.
   b. All of the parts of this chair are made of wood; therefore this chair is made of wood.
   c. All of the parts of this chair are cheap; therefore this chair is cheap.
   d. All of the players of the football team are world class; therefore the football team is world class.
   e. All of the parts of this figure are triangular; therefore this figure is triangular.
   f. This bikini bottom is blue, the bikini top is blue; therefore this bikini is blue.
2. In the following cases, are there any fallacies of unclarity or ambiguity? If so, what are these caused by?
   a. *Television presenter in interview with Mayor Koch of New York:*
      "Mr. Koch, you seem to have an endless source of income. Does that fit in with your office, and what are you doing with all that money?"
      Reply by Ed Koch: "I certainly am getting rich, and that gives me enormous satisfaction. And I am extremely socially-minded with the money: the fact is, I pay a fortune in taxes, and, all in all, the community ought to be grateful to me."
   b. *Letter to the editor:*
      The *Economist* is known as a high-quality publication. Such I can confirm, it is. During a recent solo ascent of a volcano in El Salvador, I fell and was left stranded with a compound fracture of my left leg. To support my leg so I could crawl for help, I looked around for suitable materials. Ten minutes later I set off with my lower leg surrounded by two sticks, part of a cactus and a copy of your magazine that I had been carrying with me.
      When I was rescued several hours later, the sticks and the cactus had succumbed to the rain and wear and tear. Only the magazine did not need replacing.

3. In the following excerpts, language use is discussed. Is the criticism justified? If so, which type of fallacy of unclarity or ambiguity, or other type of fallacy, has occurred?

   a. *Frida Balk-Smit Duyzentkunst on natural language and the language of arithmetic:*

   There is an enormous difference between "Two times two is four" and "2 × 2 = 4." In written form, the difference in appearance of the two sentences is clearly visible. However, when reading it out loud, the distinction is not apparent. It is probably partly because of this that we are inclined to ignore this crucial difference, which makes natural language an inexhaustible source of new information. Manifestly absurd arguments can result from this.

   A half full bottle is equal to a half empty bottle. Let's call the full bottle x and the empty bottle y. Or ½x = ½y. Multiply both sides of the equation by 2, that gives x = y. Thus, a full bottle is equal to an empty bottle.

   b. *Description of the method Kinsey used in order to learn about the sexual behavior of interviewees:*

   The interviewer should not make it too easy for the interviewee to deny the practice of a certain form of sexual activity. It is easy to say no when one is simply asked *whether* one has ever done something like that. Thus, it is assumed, as it were, that everyone has practiced every form of sexual activity. Interviewees are, therefore, asked *when* they did this or that for the first time.

4. Is Rule 7 violated in the following cases? If so, which party is responsible for this? Does the violation result from an incorrect choice of argument scheme or an incorrect application of an argument scheme?

   a. The worst antique book dealers are the ones with a personal collection. They drive me crazy when they say, "I have a book at home that you would love to have. Too bad I can't sell it to you, because it's part of my private collection."

   If a book dealer collects for himself, he shouldn't tell his customers about it. It's as if you were to go into a supermarket and there weren't any steaks. You're looking at the empty meat counter and the manager walks by. "No steaks?" you ask. "No," says the manager, "I have them all in my freezer at home."

   b. *From an advertisement by Black & Decker for a "dustbuster":*

   No other hand-held vacuum cleaner will give you greater

satisfaction than the one and only Dustbuster by Black & Decker. We don't say that without reason of course. We know that one million British families agree with us; for this is the number of Dustbusters used daily in the UK.

c. I was dead set against Darwinism. I had the feeling that it made everything meaningless and vulgar. It simply couldn't be true. If it were true I didn't want to go on living. I didn't want to have anything to do with a world like that.

d. *Letter to the editor:*

It is not widely known that the sudden appearance of the "advisory" in weather forecasts is the beginning of a movement to end the unacceptable noun domination of our language.

Soon the "advisory" will be joined by other "admonitories" from the severe "alarming" down to humble "careful," with a special category for weather systems that might miss our shores altogether, the "hopefully." The weather itself will become the "atmospherical" and a forecast will become a "before."

Once it has been demonstrated that other parts of speech can do the job of any noun, we can look forward to a new age of openness in language, when words, no longer constricted by hidebound grammatical stereotyping, are free to fulfil their true potential wherever in the sentence they choose.

e.

Calvin and Hobbes © Watterson. Reprinted with permission of Universal Press Syndicate. All rights reserved.

5. In the following two texts the prime minister accuses the interviewer of a fallacy. Do you think the accusations are correct?

a. *Interviewer:*

What do you think of the national union leader?

PM: I believe he is trying with perfect sincerity to do what he can in his members' interests.

Interviewer: Praise indeed.

PM: Yes, well, praise ... that's what *you* may call it.

b. *PM:* The socialists never fulfil their promises, always break agreements and are constantly contradicting themselves.

Interviewer: You think the socialists are undependable.

PM: That is *your* way of putting it.

6. Are discussion rules violated in the following excerpts? If so, which fallacy has been committed?

a. Waiters at Britain's Indian restaurants have been branded "miserable gits" by the editor-in-chief of the curry industry's own bible, Iqbal Wahhab. He says they make dining out more like going to a funeral. At the moment, he complains, nothing typifies the Indian restaurant experience as much as the surly, miserable waiter. "Walk into an Indian restaurant, no matter how posh, and more likely than not you will be greeted by a miserable git. It's as if his day's been ruined by your arrival."

Jim Ainsworth, editor of the *Good Food Guide*, accused Mr. Wahhab of making "silly comments." His article brought mixed response from Indian waiters around the country, one of them said Mr. Wahhab was the miserable git.

Wahed Ali, aged 22, from Bournemouth said: "The guy must have had a bad experience but it's nonsense to brand everyone with the same label. There's a miserable git in every kind of industry but you don't have to put down everyone." Iqbal Chowdhury, 45, from York said: "Mr. Wahhab just wants to show he is the Tandoori king and he should stop criticizing others who just do their job." Kuti Miah, managing partner in a Southampton restaurant said: "I went to a Thai restaurant the other night and the bloke who served me was so unfriendly."

b. *PM John Major:* "They would not be privatizing in Latin America today, if we had not first done it here. They would not be cutting high tax rates in India today, if we had not first done it here. They would not be planning to bring Eastern Europe into the Community today, if we had not first suggested it here."

c. *Text on a banner during a pro country side demonstration in London:*
Eat British lamb
40,000 foxes can't be wrong

d. *William Albright:* "Every human group is born, grows, declines and dies, as it must if it is an aggregation of individual living beings."

e. Miracles are impossible, for they cannot happen.

f. In case any of your readers take Beatrix Campbell seriously, may I point out that I have never advocated that women should "withdraw from the labor market."

   Instead, I have said that public policy should assist women to choose whether to go out to work or look after their children at home, rather than direct them into one course or the other. And yes, it's important that men should both work and marry, since mothers—including working mothers—and their children need committed fathers for financial, practical and emotional support.

g. *Advertisement:*
   America loves Burger King.

h. *Paul:* Do you believe in immortality?
   Ann: I have not sufficient data not to believe it.

i. Joe McCarthy had 81 case histories of persons who he considered communists in the state department. Of one case he said: "I do not have much information on this except the general statement of the agency that there is nothing in the files to disprove his communist connections."

j. On hearing of the death of a neighbor, somebody exclaims, "What else could you expect? A mirror was broken in that house less than a year ago."

k.

Calvin and Hobbes © Watterson. Reprinted with permission of Universal Press Syndicate. All rights reserved.

l. Rationality and analytical ability cannot be viewed as male attributes. If we were to regard them as such, we would unintentionally be giving men an advantage in job applications and promotions.

m. *Frank:* "The damaging effects of pornography have not yet been proved. So, pornography is not harmful."

n. The consequences of that suggestion (that measures designed to curb sex tourism actually work to the disadvantage of the prostitutes themselves) are clear. Sex tourism should not be discouraged but in fact even be promoted, because it creates employment opportunities in Third World countries. Maybe we should allocate some of our development aid to this effort ...

And there's no need to limit the application of this reasoning to the Third World. Here in Europe we have high unemployment too. Promoting prostitution is a way of increasing job opportunities. And to take it one step further: the crime rate reduces employment opportunities for police, while measures to reduce child abuse take away the jobs of social workers.

o. Some complaints about advertisements are ridiculous. For instance, someone responded to the advertising slogan "Modern people shop at Harrods" by saying: "I am offended, since I don't shop at Harrods, and that must mean that I am old-fashioned."

p. Millions of people watch David Letterman's late night show. Letterman gets extremely high ratings. So his show must be very good.

q. Freedom of speech is good for the country, because it is in the interest of the community that everyone has the right to say what he or she wants to say.

r. *Talk show host to one of his guests:* "Now tell me, is it first or second nature to you to tell lies?"

7. Give an analysis and evaluation of the text "Exploring Space: A Human Need" by answering questions 1–7.

1. Which proposition is the bone of contention in the text? Which roles do the parties in the dispute assume? Which type of dispute is being confronted?

2. State precisely (by referring to line numbers) how the various dialectical stages are represented in the text.

3. State the main arguments the author puts forward for his standpoint and the subarguments supporting these main arguments directly. Represent the structure of the main ar-

guments and the subarguments schematically. Justify your analysis.

4. Give an analysis of the argumentation structure of paragraph 6.

5. Identify two different types of argument schemes that are employed in the text. Justify your analysis. Answer the appropriate critical questions.

6. Identify three violations of the burden-of-proof rule (rule 2). Indicate precisely (referring to line numbers) where they occur and explain why these moves are fallacious.

7. Identify four other fallacies. Indicate precisely where they occur and explain why these moves are fallacious.

Exploring Space: A Human Need

Somewhere in the cold desolation near the south pole of Mars, apparently oblivious to the frantic efforts of earthlings to contact it, there is a lost spacecraft. We may never know what went wrong on the Mars Polar Lander, on Monday December
5   6. But what we do know is that we lost $165 million. The gloom at NASA is thick because in September the lander's companion craft, Mars Climate Orbiter, which cost $125 million was also lost as it approached the planet. Those who love to criticize NASA already are leaping on this apparent failure. The
10 complaint is familiar: The agency is being mismanaged. The agency is incompetent. The agency should be killed.

Certain irresponsible congressmen called NASA's Mars project "a waste of public funds." Some of them already vented their ideas about budget cuts. I think that in spite of
15 our recent little set back, NASA should receive even more government funding to continue its space program.

The NASA program is of paramount importance to society. We all know that exploring space is a cultural activity which adds meaning to our lives. We go into space because man is cu-
20 rious by nature. We wonder if life also arose elsewhere or if we earthlings are alone in the Universe.

If we give up the exploration of space, the next step will be to give up other government funded science programs, because they are not profitable.

Furthermore, in an age when we are left without heroes, a   25
goal-oriented space program gives the youth of the world a
dream. Besides, one can never conquer "Space," only land! In
order to grow to be citizens of the universe, we need to start
somewhere. Mars is the logical baby step before other planets.

Apart from these social advantages there are a great many   30
economical benefits to the Mars project. The employment opportunities that are created will attract a larger segment of the
student population to the sciences. A number of these will
branch out into projects of their own, compounding the benefit
by bolstering an industry of sciences. And more importantly,   35
there are many spin-offs like Teflon™ and microwave ovens.
According to many manufacturers, without the space program,
those products would never have been invented. And finally
there is, of course, the possibility of mining in space.

Some readers may respond that this might be true but then,   40
NASA projects are still too expensive. I am so bloody sick of
bleeding hearts who seize every opportunity to characterize
our efforts in space as some sort of colossal waste of cash. I
don't know where they get this idea that a great percentage of
our tax dollars was lost this year when the two Mars missions   45
failed. The entire NASA budget amounts to less than one percent of the annual federal spending. Nobody is going to convince me that earmarking this rather insubstantial amount of
money for the poor, the environment, the schools, or whatever
'cause celebre' of the week you choose, will lead to any useful   50
results in these already heavily-funded areas. That kind of aid
is not going to make a difference.

What is tragic, is that the outrage concerning the loss of a
few hundred million dollars in the space program does not
lead to the outrage with regard to the loss of billions of dollars   55
for the laughing stock F117, the "stealth" jet which appeared
on Yugoslavia's air defense radar and was shut down by an
obsolete Soviet-made SAM.

What would life be like if the complete NASA budget had
been spent on improving the quality of life in the United   60
States? It goes without saying that even more government bu-
reaucrats would have been hired, more money would have
been spent on initiatives that make problems worse. At any
rate we would have found ourselves far more ignorant of our
place in the universe than we already are.   65

Will we ever know what happened to the Mars Polar Lander? Maybe 30, 50 or a hundred years from now. Sometime in the future earthlings will be exploring Mars and stumble across the lander. We can't stop our exploration now.

Houston, Robert Wilford

8. Give an analysis and evaluation of the text "Do the Crime, Serve the Time: Juvenile Justice" by answering questions 1–8.

   1. Which proposition is the bone of contention in the text? Which roles do the parties in the dispute assume? Which type of dispute is being confronted?

   2. State precisely (by referring to line numbers) how the various dialectical stages are represented in the text.

   3. State the main arguments the author puts forward for her standpoint and the subarguments that directly support these main arguments. Represent the structure of the main arguments and the subarguments schematically. Justify your analysis.

   4. Give an analysis of the argumentation structure of paragraph 3 "The major argument ... would do it again."

   5. Identify two different types of argument schemes that are employed in the text. Justify your analysis. Answer the appropriate critical questions to determine the strength of the argumentation.

   6. Identify three violations of the burden-of-proof rule. Indicate precisely (referring to line numbers) where they occur and explain why these moves are fallacious.

   7. Identify four other fallacies not mentioned above (in your answer to question 5 or 6). Indicate precisely where they occur and explain why these moves are fallacious.

   8. Provide a brief evaluation of the quality of Cassidy's arguments. Justify this evaluation.

Do the Crime, Serve the Time: Juvenile Justice

Violence by juvenile offenders is increasing in record proportions. In the last two weeks alone, a troubled 12-year-old in Atlanta was charged with juvenile murder in the shooting death

of his 10-year-old cousin. The offender taunted his 6-year-old
cousin and her 10-year-old brother with a handgun for hours 5
until he finally removed the safety and fired a single bullet
into the 10-year-old's forehead at point blank range. In Pennsylvania, a 12-year-old has been accused of stabbing a neighbor in her home as one of her three young children watched
part of the deadly attack. In Michigan, an 11-year-old boy was 10
sentenced for shooting another boy outside a convenience
store and when asked if he was sorry was quoted as saying, "It
ain't any big deal—the motherf---er looked at me like you
shouldn't look and I ain't gonna take the sort of f---ing bullshit
from some dumb f---er." 15

This crime wave has started a debate about the appropriate punishment for juvenile criminals. Currently, the status
quo in most states, supported by the politicians who want to
maintain a liberal image, dictates juvenile offenders under
the age of 14 should not be tried nor sentenced as adults and 20
instead be treated as "children" and receive lighter sentences, probation, counseling, drug treatment, tutoring, or
incarceration in comfortable youth detention centers until
their 18th birthday when, once again, they will be released
again into society. These laws clearly reflect an outmoded le- 25
gal system where the most serious crimes committed by juveniles were joyriding and shoplifting. In today's society,
where everyone can see the most common juvenile crimes
are armed robbery, aggravated assault, and premeditated
murder, this kind of special treatment is utter nonsense. The 30
punishment for juvenile offenders should fit the viciousness
of the crime, not the age of the violent offender. As a society,
we cannot show any sympathy for, or accept any excuses
from, the young thugs, perverts, and psychopaths who are
destroying our schools and neighborhoods. 35

The major argument to have special sentencing for juvenile
offenders rests on the assumption that juveniles can not ac-
knowledge the consequences of their actions like adults can.
However, psychologists and pediatricians argue children as
young as 8 can form the intention to commit a crime. Children 40
by nature are capable of forming intent. Mr. Bart Garrison, a
columnist from the *Washington Post* agrees: "Maybe in the past
children were more naïve and innocent, but this is simply not
the case anymore. Children mature faster and in doing so, act
in every way like miniature adults." In addition, cases like 45

that of William Jennings, the 13-year-old boy from Massachu-
setts who grabbed a butcher knife and went on a bloody mid-
night rampage, fatally stabbing his father and wounding his
sister and his two nieces before he was finally subdued, all
50 over a cut in his allowance, illustrate the capacity of juveniles
to understand the consequences of crime. During his criminal
hearing he showed no remorse and said his father deserved
what was coming to him and that he would do it again.

Apart from that, appropriate sentencing of juveniles can be
55 a deterrent to crime. According to police investigators, crimi-
nologists, and many experts in the judicial system, if children
felt they would be punished for their crimes, they would be
less likely to engage in crime overall. According to Dr. Sam
Pullman from the Justice Department, "children look to their
60 peers to see what to do and how to act; if they see that their
peers are being punished for engaging in inappropriate behavior, they will be less likely to follow the path of crime."

Lastly, instituting sentences that fit the crime regardless of
the age of the criminal would set a precedent that the Ameri-
65 can judicial system is tough on crime which is something the
vast majority of the American public desires. With incidents
like the fatal shooting at Columbine High School and juvenile
crime on the rise in general, the American government needs
to stop listening to the pathetic "criminals are people too"
70 whiners and send a message that this sort of behavior will not
be tolerated, nor condoned.

The first lesson that should be taught in school is: You do
the crime, you serve the time. The current policy just doesn't
work. If these bleeding heart liberals want to keep this policy,
75 they need to show America how this policy is effective. Parents, teachers, and society as a whole will not enjoy peace of
mind until our schools and streets are free of violent juveniles.

Ellen Cassidy, Tucson, AZ

SPECIAL ASSIGNMENT 6

Give an analysis and an evaluation of the text "What is Beeren
Afraid Of?" by answering questions 1–7. The assignment should
be handed in at the next class meeting. In the following class

meeting, the instructor will discuss the assignment; the students will receive individual comments on their assignments.

1. Which proposition(s) is (are) the bone of contention in the text? Which roles do the parties in the dispute assume? Of which type is the dispute?
2. State precisely (by referring to line numbers) how the dialectical stages are represented in the text.
3. State the *main* arguments which the author puts forward for her standpoint(s). Give, in addition, a schematic overview of the argumentation structure of these main arguments and justify your analysis.
4. Give a schematic overview of the argumentation structure of paragraph 7. In addition, make three unexpressed premises explicit.
5. Identify two different types of argument schemes in paragraph 7. Explain your analysis. Answer the appropriate critical questions for both schemes.
6 Identify one violation of discussion rule 2 (the burden-of-proof rule) and one violation of discussion rule 6 (the starting point rule).
7. Identify three other violations of discussion rules in the text. Indicate where they occur and explain why these moves are fallacious.

WHAT IS BEEREN AFRAID OF?
Marliese Griffith-van den Berg

An article by Marliese Griffith-van den Berg, who is head restorer in the Fitzwilliam Museum in Cambridge, was published in the British newspaper The Independent. *In this article she gave a detailed analysis of the opinions with regard to Goldreyer's restoration of Barnett Newman's painting* Who's Afraid of Red Yellow and Blue III. *In a letter to Wim Beeren, the director of the Stedelijk Museum in Amsterdam, Griffith-van den Berg explains why she believes that Goldreyer has not restored the painting correctly and why Beeren, in her view, is responsible for the mistakes made.*

Dear Wim,
In the restoration studio at the Fitzwilliam Museum in Cambridge, we have been closely following the debate sur-

rounding the unfortunate restoration of Barnett Newman's
Who's Afraid of Red Yellow and Blue III; each day, I gave a report
5 to my English colleagues, on the basis of articles from Dutch
newspapers, of the most recent developments in the affair.
Our involvement in the debate grew day by day as a result
and, with the encouragement of my colleagues, I had an article published in *The Independent* in which I expressed my view
10 of the affair; an article that also caused quite a stir in the Netherlands.

After having carefully analyzed the facts regarding the restoration, I believe that there are two important matters that
deserve particular attention in the debate. The first concerns
15 your being in the wrong when you say that Newman's painting has been correctly restored; the second implies (however
unpleasant it is for me to have to say this) that you are responsible for the mistakes made. Although both of these standpoints are connected, it seems to me to be useful for the clarity
20 of the discussion (they do, in fact, refer to separate subjects) to
justify them individually.

There are four good reasons for my first point. One: reliable
research by the Central Laboratory in Amsterdam has shown
that Newman executed his painting with a brush and that he
25 used oil paint; in his restoration, Goldreyer has used a paint
roller and Magna, an acrylic paint. In good restorations, however, as you know, only the same paint is used as was used in
the original, or (if that paint is difficult to remove) a paint that
is easier to remove in future restorations. You can take it from
30 me that the latter does not apply to Magna. It is, after all, pa-
tently obvious that a top coat of acrylic paint cannot be removed without causing damage to the original layer of paint.

Second: according to the international code of restorers,
only damaged sections may be retouched in a restoration.
35 Goldreyer has, however, completely repainted the red section
of the painting, something which has emerged from the inspection of the painting by Professor Ernst van de Wetering.
He found craquelures only in the blue and in the yellow sections of the painting and not in the red, which indicates that
40 the red section has been completely repainted.

Three: a good restoration ought to be preceded by detailed
research. This did not take place in Goldreyer's restoration.
There is, in any case, no one who can prove (by means of pho-
tographs, reports and such like) that any research was carried

out. Let us be honest, therefore, and conclude that no research 45
whatsoever was carried out.

Four: I am not alone in my opinion that the painting has not
been restored in a correct manner. My colleagues are of exactly
the same opinion and there are also a great many restorers, art
experts and other interested persons in the Netherlands who 50
have made it known that they cannot agree with the result of
Goldreyer's work.

Then the second point: why do I think that you are personally responsible for the mistakes made in the restoration? Directly after the attack on the painting, you invited an 55
international group of restorers to discuss the problems of the
restoration. The head restorer at the Stedelijk, Elisabeth
Bracht, and I myself were also present. It was agreed then that
the treatment of the painting would remain within the bounds
of the international code of restorers. Nevertheless, you then 60
sent the work to Goldreyer in New York, without stating precisely how he was to proceed in the restoration. You did not,
therefore, keep to your agreement. You have also been negli-
gent: you failed to set up a committee to keep a close track of
Goldreyer's work and to direct the restoration. With such a 65
committee, Goldreyer would, of course, never have had the
chance to use acrylic paint and he would never have been able
to "re-roll" the entire red section. Moreover, you paid no heed
to good and sound advice. For example, you ignored my advice to require Goldreyer to make video recordings of the res- 70
toration and to have these viewed each week by experts; I
believe you considered that to be rather patronizing. And
when Elisabeth Bracht reported to you from New York that
Goldreyer was repainting the work, you responded with a sar-
castic remark and you didn't really want to listen. 75

Wim, if it had been only one of these things, then you might
still have been forgiven; after all, everyone makes a mistake
now and then. But so many mistakes together, you really do
have to be blamed for that. You would be well advised to admit that the restoration is a fiasco and you ought to assume the 80
responsibility for the mistakes made.

For some weeks now, I have been wondering why you are
so afraid to admit that the restoration has been unsuccessful
and that you have made mistakes in the procedure. Do you
stick to your opinion merely because you think that by doing 85
so you won't have to suffer any loss of face? Or did you, by any

chance, deliberately allow the restoration to be carried out in this way? Perhaps because, as a devotee of and expert on conceptual art (and Newman's painting wasn't that) you are under the impression that all art is reproducible?

III

Presentation

9

Written Argumentation

Putting together a convincing argumentative text requires an attitude conducive to resolving the difference of opinion concerned. Besides structuring the argumentation appropriately and making sure that it is sound in every respect, it is also important to present one's case well. In this endeavor, it is usually best to alternate explicit formulations of arguments and standpoints with implicit ones. First of all, it is good to realize that an analytical overview of the argumentation structure is a useful analytic tool for writing and rewriting the text.

9.1   A WELL-WRITTEN ARGUMENTATIVE TEXT

The most important thing, not only in analyzing and evaluating argumentation, but also in presenting an argument, is reasonableness. A reasonable argument contains nothing that would, by definition, form an obstacle to the resolution of a difference of opinion. When presenting a case, it must be kept in mind that the argumentation is part of a discussion with another party, even when this is only implicitly so. The argumentation must convince readers by removing their doubts or by responding adequately to their criticisms.

An argument is an attempt to change the audience's mind. Because reasonable argumentation must not have any fallacies in it, the rules for critical discussions also serve as useful guidelines for how to present a case. Among other things, they recommend not to put words in the other party's mouth and give a careful interpretation of what they have to say. The other party's words should not be taken out of context, nor should the arguer try to trick or deceive.

To reach resolution, the argumentation must also be comprehensible to the intended audience. This means that the various parts of the argumentative text should be put together coherently. The use of language should be as clear and understandable as possible. Of course this does not mean that one should try to ingratiate oneself with the reader. This will have as little chance of success as boasting or trying to be the funniest guy in town. The best advice is to follow the rules for communication: Keep to the point, don't beat around the bush, say clearly what you mean, give all the information required for understanding the argument, and be concise.

If written argumentation is well presented, the reader will not miss any of the important points. For this, it is a minimal requirement that the standpoint and arguments be expressed clearly. This does not necessarily mean they should be formulated explicitly—that would be unnatural and irritating and sound stilted and pedantic. A well-presented argument will have a good balance of explicit and implicit elements.

If it is already obvious that the arguments being presented are intended to defend a certain standpoint, then it is not necessary to label them explicitly as such—for instance, if a standpoint is presented that is very surprising or extreme then everybody knows that what follows is going to be a defense of it. But sometimes it is not clear what is the standpoint and what is the argument:

> Elaine is very particular. She's always on time.

Two interpretations of this are possible:

a   Elaine is very particular. So she's always on time.
b   Elaine is very particular. We know that, because she's always on time.

It is a good idea, when writing out the first draft of an argumentative text, to label the standpoint and the arguments explicitly. In a later version, the text can be made more natural by replacing unnecessarily explicit parts with implicit or indirect phrasing. A series of statements and claims can be livened up considerably by throwing in an occasional rhetorical question, an exclamation, or some other expression of feeling, as in *b*:

a It is very peculiar that the director chose a world-famous actor for the role of the father in this film, and a big waste of money and talent, because after just ten minutes the father dies.
b What director would choose a world-famous actor for the role of the father in this film? After just ten minutes the father dies. What a waste of money and talent!

9.2   AN ANALYTICAL OVERVIEW AS AN AID TO WRITING

Generally an analytical overview is made only after an argumentative text is completed. But it can also be a useful tool when rewriting the text or even when writing the first draft. An analytical overview brings together concisely all the information necessary for evaluating an argumentative text, that is, what is the difference of opinion to be resolved, what is the structure of the argumentation, and so on. The analytical overview can be used to check whether the argumentation can stand up to criticism. If weaknesses are found, the argumentation can be adjusted or expanded. Once the analytical overview is shaped up, it makes a useful guide for writing an improved version of the argument.

It is also possible to write out an argumentative text based on an analytical overview that is made especially for that purpose; such an overview consists of an outline of the arguments to be presented. The overview makes it easier to write the text so that it clearly expresses the structure of the argumentation. Naturally, the overview should formulate the difference of opinion unambiguously and state who the parties to the discussion are and what positions they are taking.

The reasons for presenting an argument can vary. Sometimes the text is a response to someone else's argument. This is clearly a discussion situation, with a specific opponent whom one is trying to convince. Other times, writers feel inclined to present their standpoint even though they have no idea what others will think of it.

There are two positions to adopt when responding to the standpoint and arguments of another party. One position is to take the opposite standpoint, in which case a mixed difference of opinion arises. The other position is merely to point out weak parts of the other party's argumentation to show that it is not sound, in which case no attempt is made to adopt the opposite standpoint.

The analytical overview must state exactly what standpoint is being attacked or defended, and the other party's standpoint must be as fairly and as completely stated as possible. After that, one's own arguments are summed up, taking into account potential criticism from the opponent. The best way to sum up the arguments is in a diagram showing the structure of the argumentation to be used: This makes clear how the arguments are related. If the text is a response to someone else's argumentation, then it is useful to make a similar diagram of the other party's argumentation: This makes it easier to identify which parts of the argumentation should be responded to.

A diagram outlining argumentation structure is given in chapter 5 for the peace demonstration example. Unexpressed premises are not included in this diagram. Sometimes it is a good idea to include them, for instance if they are links in the argumentation that are unclear or even suspect. When an unexpressed premise is supported by yet another argument, it must always be explicitly included in the analytical overview. If the unexpressed premise is not made explicit, then it may be unclear where the argument belongs.

9.3   QUALITY CONTROL

Argumentation not only needs to be structured well but should also be sound. In checking this, the analytical overview can be a useful tool. Its outline of essential elements makes it easier to check systematically for fallacies and for logical or pragmatic inconsistencies. It is also useful in checking whether the reasoning is valid, whether appropriate argument schemes have been used, and (by raising the relevant critical questions) whether they have been correctly applied.

Using the analytical overview, the argumentation should be checked carefully to see whether it takes into account potential doubts or objections from the reader. If these have not been taken into account, then it is a good idea to add new arguments or to expand or further support existing arguments. Only if the analytical overview is satisfactory is there a good chance that the text written from it will meet the aim of the argument, that is, to resolve a difference of opinion with the reader.

What follows is the first draft of a student's text and a demonstration of how an analytical overview can be used to improve it:

Ban Commercial Health Care

Private clinics would seem to be a good investment, if you look at how fast their number is growing. But whether they will be successful remains to be seen. Besides being unprofitable, they are only available to well-to-do people. Since these clinics are commercial, the service they provide depends on their profitability. The quality of the treatment therefore depends on its price, even though one of the main principles of our welfare state is that social provisions should be equally available to all. In my opinion private clinics should be incorporated into existing hospital partnerships.

In the first place, hospitals are suffering from competition from private clinics. The clinics have forced hospitals to specialize and to buy the necessary equipment for this, while at the same time employment in hospitals has decreased. This is all caused by private clinics taking over the minor procedures, while the more difficult and much less frequent major operations are all done by hospitals. Our health care law prohibits patients staying in a clinic more than 24 hours.

Secondly, inequality has arisen in health care provided to rich and poor. Private clinics are only available to people in higher income groups, because health insurance does not reimburse treatment in private clinics.

Finally, the quality of care in private clinics is not as good as that in hospitals. Because of carelessness and too many operations, the quality has eroded. After all, quality control in private clinics is almost impossible. Medical associations have no say in the clinics, there is no peer review, and profit-making plays too large a role.

It would be wise to incorporate the clinics into existing hospital partnerships. This decommercializing measure would improve the functioning of hospitals, the availability of the clinics, and the quality of health care.

In Figure 9.1, you will find an analytical overview of this text.

Evaluation of "Ban Commercial Health Care"

From the title and the general drift of the argumentation, it can be deduced that the author finds it undesirable to allow commercial private clinics. From the way the standpoint is formulated, it appears that the author wants to end this situation by means of a specific action: incorporating private clinics into existing hospital partnerships. The arguments presented are all aimed at showing that there are significant drawbacks to private clinics. The author does not ex-

---

a   **The difference of opinion**

Single nonmixed disagreement:

Author: positive standpoint with regard to the proposition "Private
          clinics should be incorporated into existing hospital partnerships."

Readers: (presumably) doubt this standpoint.

FIG. 9.1a.   Analytical overview of "Ban commercial health care." The difference of opinion.

plain why his or her solution is the best one. The arguments, in fact,
support a different standpoint (The existence of private clinics is undesirable) than the one the author suggests he or she is defending
(Private clinics should be incorporated into existing hospital partnerships). The author is therefore guilty of the fallacy of *ignoratio
elenchi*.

The standpoint the author is actually defending is indicated in the
first paragraph: "Whether they will be successful remains to be
seen." But this formulation is not very clear: It suggests that the clinics haven't attracted many clients, whereas the rest of the arguments
aim to show that the clinics are undesirable (regardless of how many
clients they have). The only other reference to the unpopularity of the
clinics is the passing remark in the first paragraph that so far the clinics are unprofitable.

Already in the first paragraph, arguments are given for the standpoint that private clinics are undesirable ("Besides being unprofitable ... should be equally available to all"). However, the
presentation suggests that the argumentation only begins in the second paragraph, which starts with "in the first place," followed by an
argument. For this reason, the arguments given in the introductory
paragraph are not included in the analytical overview.

What is more, the argumentation in the first paragraph is confusing. Clearly the author is critical of the commercial nature of private
clinics, but it is less clear why he is. What exactly is the problem? Is it

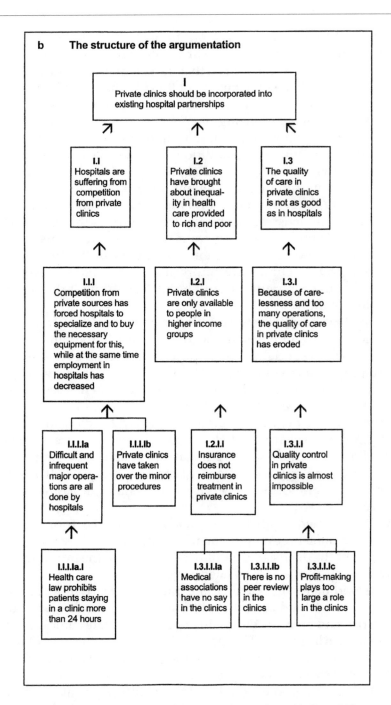

b   The structure of the argumentation

I
Private clinics should be incorporated into existing hospital partnerships

I.I
Hospitals are suffering from competition from private clinics

I.2
Private clinics have brought about inequality in health care provided to rich and poor

I.3
The quality of care in private clinics is not as good as in hospitals

I.I.I
Competition from private sources has forced hospitals to specialize and to buy the necessary equipment for this, while at the same time employment in hospitals has decreased

I.2.I
Private clinics are only available to people in higher income groups

I.3.I
Because of carelessness and too many operations, the quality of care in private clinics has eroded

I.I.I.Ia
Difficult and infrequent major operations are all done by hospitals

I.I.I.Ib
Private clinics have taken over the minor procedures

I.2.I.I
Insurance does not reimburse treatment in private clinics

I.3.I.I
Quality control in private clinics is almost impossible

I.I.I.Ia.I
Health care law prohibits patients staying in a clinic more than 24 hours

I.3.I.I.Ia
Medical associations have no say in the clinics

I.3.I.I.Ib
There is no peer review in the clinics

I.3.I.I.Ic
Profit-making plays too large a role in the clinics

FIG. 9.1b.   Analytical overview of "Ban Commercial Health Care." The structure of the argumentation.

163

that only well-to-do people can profit from the high-quality care of the clinics, which conflicts with the principle of social provisions being equally available to all? Or is it that the commercial nature of the clinics somehow reduces the quality of the care they offer? It would seem the author holds both opinions, as both points return in the course of the argumentation (arguments 1.2 and 1.3). Actually, these arguments are not only confusingly formulated and badly placed, but they are also redundant. In addition, is it not misleading to count private clinics as belonging to "social provisions"?

The first main argument (1.1) mentioned by the author in the second paragraph for the standpoint that private clinics should be incorporated into existing hospital partnerships is that hospitals are suffering from competition from private clinics. This argument is undermined by the author's statement in the first paragraph that private clinics are unprofitable. The reader may be thinking that the competition can't be all that strong if the clinics are still losing money.

To show that hospitals are suffering from competition from private clinics, the author notes the fact that because of the clinics, hospitals have had to specialize and to purchase expensive equipment, while employment has gone down (1.1.1). It is questionable whether this argument is acceptable. Is it really true to say that it is because of private clinics that hospitals have had to specialize and to purchase expensive equipment? Or was this already a trend and the introduction of clinics merely accelerated it? After all, even if there were no private clinics, hospitals would still have to be able to perform "the more difficult and much less frequent major operations." It would appear that the author here is guilty of the fallacy of *post hoc ergo propter hoc*.

Another problem with this argument is that the formulation "while at the same time employment has decreased" does not make clear whether the decreasing employment is due to the introduction of private clinics, or is an unrelated development.

The second main argument (1.2) is rather unclearly formulated: "Private clinics have brought about inequality in health care provided to rich and poor." Is the quality of care in private clinics higher or lower than in hospitals? The first would seem to be the case. Otherwise, it would be strange to object to the fact that private clinics are only available to well-to-do patients.

The third main argument (1.3), that the quality of private clinics is not as good as in hospitals, conflicts with what is suggested in argument 1.2. The argumentation thus contains a *logical inconsistency*.

The argument in support of the third main argument, "Because of carelessness and too many operations, the quality of care in private clinics has eroded" (1.3.1), is much too strongly formulated. After all, it is not clear on what grounds the author thinks he or she can claim that the quality of private clinics has declined. And, strictly speaking, this argument does not even support the substandpoint 1.3. If the quality of private clinics was initially higher than that of hospitals, then a decline in quality does not automatically mean that the quality of care in clinics is now lower than that in hospitals. Again, this is the fallacy of *ignoratio elenchi*.

Argument 1.3.1.1, "quality control in private clinics is almost impossible," is another example of irrelevant argumentation. If quality control is not possible, then it is not possible to judge the quality of the care. The chance of poor care is indeed greater without quality control, but it is unwarranted to conclude with no additional evidence that the quality of care has indeed declined, as is done in 1.3.1. Similarly, that too many operations are performed is not supported by the quality control argument.

In support of argument 1.3.1.1, "quality control in private clinics is almost impossible," the author gives another irrelevant argument, namely, that profit-making plays too large a role in private clinics. It would seem that this argument is simply in the wrong place in the text. Although it says nothing about the possibility of quality control, it could perhaps be used to support the claim that too many operations are performed (1.3.1).

9.4   REWRITING THE TEXT

The text "Ban Commercial Health Care" has a lot of weaknesses. It has an internal contradiction, uses irrelevant arguments, and the arguments that are relevant are often unclearly formulated or do not stand up to obvious points of criticism. So there is plenty of room for improvement.

In rewriting a text, several sorts of operations may be performed. Certain parts of the text may be deleted. That is sometimes the best solution if these parts are redundant or, on second thought, appear to be untenable. Certain things may be added to make the argumentation stronger or clearer; adding more background information or expanding an argument is often a good solution. Some parts of the text may need to be rephrased, for instance, by weakening a too strongly formulated argument or by making a vague or confusing formulation more precise. Sometimes it helps to put the parts of the argumentation in a different order, thereby making it clearer how they are related to each other.

Deleting, adding, rephrasing, and reordering can improve the quality of the text and make it easier to understand. This can be demonstrated by comparing the original version of "Ban Commercial Health Care" with the following revision of it.

Revised Version of "Ban Commercial Health Care"

A   In recent years private clinics have been springing up all over. In the past five years alone, more than a thousand new clinics have been set up. The question is whether this is a good thing.

B   In the first place, hospitals are suffering a lot from competition from private clinics. Because our national health care law prohibits patients staying more than 24 hours in a clinic, private clinics have mostly taken over only the minor operations. But these are the most frequent operations. Because of this, employment in hospitals has decreased, and in spite of decreasing revenues hospitals have still had to invest in the expensive equipment needed for the more specialized operations.

C   Secondly, private clinics have rejected any form of quality control. Medical associations have no say in the clinics and there is no peer review. The risk of carelessness is particularly great in private clinics: because of their commercial nature, clinics stand to gain from the highest possible number of operations. This aim for quantity may be at the expense of quality.

D   Thirdly, the introduction of private clinics to the health care scene has brought about undesirable discrimination based on income. Private clinics are available almost exclusively to private patients from higher income groups, because insurance companies do not reimburse the costs of treatment. The inequality thus created conflicts with the principle that health care services should be equally available to everyone.

E   In my opinion there is every reason to call a halt to the commercialization of health care. Further increase in the number of private clinics is not in the interest of either hospitals or patients.

Now we can compare the two versions, noting what changes have been made and why.

Paragraph A.   The standpoint "Private clinics should be incorporated into existing hospital partnerships" has been replaced by

"Further increase in the number of private clinics is undesirable." This standpoint does not advocate taking any specific action; so now the arguments really support the standpoint.

To keep from unnecessarily weakening the competition argument (paragraph B), the mention of clinics being unprofitable has been deleted. The reference to clinics being for wealthier clients, along with the following two sentences, have been removed from the first paragraph; not only are these arguments confusingly formulated, they are not needed here, because they appear later in the text. A further result of these changes is that the argumentation now begins where it should, in paragraph B, with the phrase "In the first place."

However, all of these deletions have left paragraph A rather bare; by providing more background information, the introduction has been strengthened. The period referred to is stated, and statistics are cited on the growth in number of private clinics during this period.

Paragraph B.　In the second paragraph, the arguments have been rearranged. Originally, the argument that hospitals have suffered from competition from private clinics was supported by a series of cause-and-effect arguments which were ordered "from effect to cause." In the rewrite, the order has been turned around: Now the arguments are presented "from cause to effect." This prevents the paragraph fading away like a candle in the night; now the most important of the negative effects for hospitals is prominently positioned at the end of the paragraph.

Several sentences have been reformulated. The observation that "minor procedures are the most frequent" now receives more emphasis by being stated in a separate sentence. In the original text, this information could only indirectly be deduced from the statement that major operations were much less frequent. It is important to emphasize that private clinics have taken over the most frequent procedures because this is what makes it plausible that employment at hospitals has gone down. A further revision was to remove the suggestion that competition from clinics has forced hospitals to purchase expensive new specialized equipment. In the revised text, the problem is not that hospitals have been forced to specialize, but that the required investments have had to be made in the face of declining revenues.

Paragraph C.　The new third paragraph corresponds to the fourth paragraph in the old version. This change in order is explained under paragraph D. First, we look at the changes made to this paragraph.

The original text did not give plausible arguments for the assertion that the quality of care in private clinics is not as good as in hospitals. Therefore, this assertion has been deleted. In its place, the supporting argument about lack of quality control has been made a main argument. To emphasize the undesirability of the lack of quality control, it is now argued that the risk of carelessness is particularly great in private clinics. This argument replaces the poorly supported argument that the quality of care in private clinics has decreased.

By reordering them, the various arguments have acquired different relations. The argument that profit plays too great a role is no longer used to support the argument that quality control is almost impossible. It is now formally presented as support for the substandpoint that it is in the interest of clinics to carry out as many operations as possible. For this standpoint, it is relevant. The passage about "too many operations" has been less strongly formulated to make it easier to defend.

The result of all these changes is that "Because of carelessness and too many operations, the quality has eroded" has been replaced with "The risk of carelessness is particularly great in private clinics: Because of their commercial nature, clinics stand to gain from the highest possible number of operations. This aim for quantity may be at the expense of quality."

Paragraph D.   The danger of logical inconsistency has been reduced by placing less emphasis in the third paragraph on the lower quality of care in clinics. Nevertheless, it seems unwise to overemphasize that the introduction of private clinics in health care has given rise to "discrimination based on income." After all, paragraph C claims that the risk of carelessness is greater in private clinics. Therefore, it seems wiser to make the "discrimination" argument more a matter of principle. This is done in the rewrite of paragraph D, where it is stated that health care (whatever the quality) ought to be equally available to everyone. The order of paragraphs C and D has been reversed to remove any suggestion that "discrimination based on income" is related to a difference in quality of care. Paragraph C has already made it clear that the quality of care in clinics is not guaranteed. Discrimination in health care is rejected on grounds of principle, disregarding the question whether care in private clinics is better or worse than in hospitals.

Paragraph E.   Since the revised version has a different standpoint, the repetition of the standpoint in the closing paragraph of course also had to be changed. The most important argument for the standpoint (i.e., that further increase in the number of private clinics is undesirable) is briefly summarized here.

FURTHER READING

A useful textbook on writing argumentative texts is S. Barnet and H. Bedau, *Critical Thinking, Reading, and Writing. A Brief Guide to Argument*, Boston: St. Martin's Press, 1993. A collection of studies about argumentative (re)writing was recently published in J. Andriessen and P. Coirier (Ed.), *Foundations of Argumentative Text Processing*, Amsterdam: Amsterdam University Press, 1999.

EXERCISES

1. Rewrite the text *Why Not Dutch?* (chapter 5, special assignment 5).

SPECIAL ASSIGNMENT 7

Write an argumentative text on a subject of your own choice of approximately three pages (double spaced). At the next class meeting, one copy of the text should be submitted to the instructor, a second copy should be given to a fellow-student. This fellow-student writes a short evaluation of the text (1 page) in which he/she makes use of all the analytical instruments and evaluation procedures that have been discussed in the course. In the following meeting, one copy should be submitted to the instructor and one copy should be handed to the student whose text has been evaluated. The instructor gives some general comments.

10
Oral Argumentation

A participant in an argumentative discussion must always try to anticipate the response of the other party. The participants jointly are responsible for how the discussion proceeds and for its quality. Spurious conflicts and spurious agreements are to be avoided, the participants should respond clearly and in a relevant way to each other's arguments, they should not take on too much at once, they should not cause unnecessary delay, and they should make sure that there is a clear conclusion.

In preparing an argumentative speech, special attention should be given to an attractive introduction and a clear conclusion. It is best to give the speech by referring to notes taken from the analytical overview, sparingly supplemented by other points. The presentation of the speech must be clear and attractive and suitable to the occasion and the audience. Speakers should not turn the audience against them by giving a clumsy presentation or using stuffy language.

10.1 PREPARING FOR A DISCUSSION

In daily life, argumentation is more often presented orally than in written form. People actually spend much of their time in discus-

171

sion—not only in formal debates and other organized discussions, but also in informal talks and spontaneous conversations. Sometimes it is difficult to draw the line between an ordinary conversation and an argumentative discussion. Many conversations have both argumentative and nonargumentative elements, and in practice, the discourse may almost automatically shift from one type to the other. For some people this is a reason for complaint:

> Before you know it, every conversation turns into a debate. People can't seem to merely exchange experiences, jokes, rumors, anecdotes, and leave it at that. There's always a "Yes but …," "Well, I think that …," "That may be *your* opinion, but …," or "I don't agree."

In preparing for a discussion, a person usually does not know in advance what points the other party will put forward or exactly how the discussion will proceed. Even so, it is better not to concentrate exclusively on the points you want to present, but to think about what you can expect from the other party. What points will they present and how will they respond to your arguments? Good preparation will enable you to be flexible in responding to the other party.

The first thing is to be well prepared. This involves becoming thoroughly familiar with the topic to be discussed, weighing the pros and cons of various possible positions, and deciding which position you are going to take. What is your standpoint? What are the main arguments for it? The answers to these questions should be written up in an analytical overview; this overview will form the basis of the defense of your position.

Secondly, it is useful to anticipate what position the other party will probably take and what their background in the subject matter is. What is their standpoint likely to be? What arguments might they use? What objections might they raise against your arguments? If you do not know who the other party will be, it is harder to guess, but it is still useful to think what objections might be made to your standpoint and your arguments.

If you do not expect strong opposition to your standpoint, then you can spend most of your preparation time on making your defense as strong as possible. Just as in preparing a written presentation, the analytical overview can help you to check your own arguments and see where they need to be improved. You can think of objections that may be made and how you might respond to them. These responses can be jotted down in the overview next to the relevant argument. Sometimes, rather than waiting for your opponent, you can just as well present the objection yourself and counter it:

> Of course I am aware that ... but ...
>
> One possible disadvantage of my proposed solution is that ... But it seems to me the advantages more than outweigh it because ...

If you expect your standpoint to meet with strong resistance, then you will want to spend considerable time anticipating the position of your opponents and the arguments they might use. If you have no information on what their position will be, then you can work on thinking of arguments that would support the standpoint opposite to yours. You can make an analytical overview of that, and then go through it and think how you could respond to each of the arguments. Some of these responses you may decide to incorporate in your own presentation, whereas the others can be held ready for use during the discussion.

One result of your preparation will be an analytical overview that includes not only your own standpoint and the arguments for it, but also your responses to objections the other party may raise and, if necessary, your own reactions to arguments and standpoints of the other party. An outline version of this analytical overview can serve as the basis for your part in the discussion.

10.2 PARTICIPATING IN A DISCUSSION

It is in the interest of participants who sincerely want to resolve a difference of opinion that the discussion proceed efficiently. With or without the aid of a chairperson, the participants together decide how the discussion will proceed. Their responsibility begins with their use of language. To prevent misunderstandings, both parties must express their intentions as clearly as possible and interpret the opponent's statements as accurately as possible. This is especially important during the confrontation stage. Misunderstandings in this stage can result in disagreements that are merely verbal and not real disagreements. In such a situation, the participants actually hold the same opinion, but talk at cross purposes because they define the standpoint in different ways.

An example of a verbal disagreement is if one party claims to reject socialism, and the other party claims to support socialism, while they each define socialism differently: One equates it with communism and the other with social democracy. In fact, both agree that communism is bad and social democracy is good. In a case like this, *precization* is needed. This means considering various possible interpretations of a statement and then choosing one of them. In the following exchange, Ronald explains more precisely what he means by *musical* when it becomes clear that the use of that word has led to misunderstanding:

> Ronald: I think Peter is very musical.
>
> Martha: But I've never heard him play a single note!
>
> Ronald: When I say he's "musical" I don't mean he has talent for playing an instrument, but that he has feeling for music and perfect pitch.

To ensure that they are both talking about the same thing, the participants may decide to assign *definitions* to the main terms relevant to the discussion. The definition agreed on may be one of the meanings the word has in everyday language, or it may be an unusual or technical meaning. In the latter case, the definition chosen must fit in with the aim of the discussion. It is not allowable for one party to insist on a certain definition just because it makes that party's position easier to defend.

Talking at cross purposes may not only lead to a spurious disagreement, but may also result in a spurious agreement, so that discussion of the real difference of opinion does not take place. The author of the following text seems to be of the opinion that spurious resolutions are the main cause of the failure of discussions:

> In Dutch discussions everybody always agrees with everybody else. There is never any real debate … Dutch discussions, in short, are not the solution to the problem but the problem itself, because discussions ending in unanimous agreement are always suspect.

The actual discussion can only begin after it has been established that there really is a difference of opinion, what exactly the points of disagreement are, and what positions the participants are taking. To ensure the discussion proceeds in an orderly manner, the participants need to observe a number of important rules, including the following ones.

1. Each point raised in the discussion must be relevant to the matter at hand at that moment. There is no use in advancing solu-

tions before the problem has been clarified, nor is there any use in presenting essential information after a decision has already been made. Participants must speak only if they really have something to say and, at the same time, must not refrain from raising a relevant point.

2. It is best to avoid making too many points at once. The discussion can quickly become chaotic. Instead of presenting six points, it is better to start with one or two. Participants should restrict themselves to a couple of important points and not bring up side issues and minor details.
3. The function of each contribution must be clear. Why is the speaker responding as she is? Is she trying to set something straight? Is she offering supplementary evidence or an explanation? Is she presenting an alternative solution?
4. Participants should not draw out the discussion by unnecessary repetition or by bringing up points that have already been dealt with.
5. The discussion must be brought to a clear conclusion. It must be perfectly clear whether the difference of opinion has been resolved, and if so, what the resolution is. The consequences of the resolution must also be made clear. Should the agreement be reported to a certain organization? Do further steps need to be taken?

10.3 PREPARING AN ARGUMENTATIVE SPEECH

Speeches and lectures often contain argumentative sections. Just as in written argumentation, though, an oral presentation can be considered argumentative only if it reflects a situation where two parties have different opinions. An argumentative speech serves a purpose only if the standpoint to be defended is controversial and of sufficient interest to the intended audience. If possible, speakers should find that out beforehand. They should formulate their standpoint as clearly as possible. The scope of it must be clear: Does the proposition involve only certain persons or aspects or does it apply to everyone and everything? Non-falsifiable labels like "by nature" should be avoided, as they make it difficult to refute the standpoint. Any terms that may be wrongly interpreted should be precisely defined.

In preparing their speech, speakers may find it helpful to order the arguments they intend to use in an analytical overview. Instead of rattling off a whole series of arguments, it is better to stick to just a few strong arguments, work them out well, and support them convincingly. The analytical overview, then, schematically represents the heart of the speech.

A speech usually involves more than just argumentation, however. Normally it starts with an introduction, in which the speaker tries to rouse the audience's attention for what he or she wants to say. Then the speaker provides necessary background information and only after that does the argumentation itself begin. The speaker presents arguments in support of his or her standpoint and may also attempt to counter certain objections that might be made to the case. At the end of the speech, the speaker repeats the standpoint and perhaps summarizes the most important arguments.

The introduction must be interesting enough to gain the audience's attention. There are many ways to do this. The speaker may relate a personal experience, a surprising quotation, or an interesting anecdote. He or she may refer to a current event or a well-known historical incident. Raising a concrete question that the audience finds important is also a good way to get the listeners involved. Of course, there needs to be a clear connection between the introduction and the argumentation that follows.

Normally the standpoint to be defended should be stated in the introduction. The speaker explains what he or she is going to talk about and what position is taken. If the speaker expects the standpoint to meet with strong resistance, then it may be wise to first mention the arguments and lead the audience step by step to the conclusion. If it is a long speech, it may be useful to close the introduction with a brief outline of what will follow. This gives listeners a good idea of what is in store for them.

If the speaker is not only giving arguments for his or her own standpoint but also giving arguments against the opposite standpoint, then this speaker must decide in what order to do this. The most common order is to show first why the opponent's standpoint is untenable, and then to give arguments for one's own standpoint. But it is also possible to reverse the order. As long as the argumentation does not become confusing, it is even possible to alternate parts of the defense with parts of the attack. When defending one's own standpoint it is advisable to give the strongest arguments either right at the beginning or at the end. What comes first will influence the reception of the rest, and what comes last will be remembered the best.

The conclusion of a speech should plant the most important points firmly in the minds of the audience. No new points should be brought up at this time, nor should the complete argument be repeated. It is important that the conclusion be clear and attractive. A nice touch is to refer back to the introduction, creating the impression of a well-rounded whole.

In situations where every word counts or where there is a strict time limit, it may be necessary to write out the entire speech. In doing this, the speaker should remember to use language that will sound natural when spoken aloud and to practice reading aloud with expression. Ordinarily, instead of writing it all out, it is better to just write down the main points of the speech. If speakers choose their words at the moment of speaking, their speech will sound livelier and more natural.

An inexperienced speaker should write out the introduction and the conclusion in full and put all the main arguments into an analytical overview. Sentences that mark the transition from one passage to another, for instance, those announcing an argument or giving short summaries, should also be written out. If this is not done, there is some danger that the thread of the argument will be lost in the heat of the debate, so that the audience cannot follow the speaker's train of thought.

10.4   PRESENTING AN ARGUMENTATIVE SPEECH

A speech must be presented clearly so that the audience can easily follow the speaker's train of thought. The audience must not become bored. That is why the speaker must also make sure that the speech is pleasant to listen to.

The speech should be suitable to both the occasion and the audience. If the audience consists of laypeople, it is no good giving technical explanations or using technical vocabulary, whereas for an audience of specialists in the field, this is just what is required. As far as the style of the speech, a formal occasion, such as a court case or a meeting of parliament, requires more formal phrasing than would be appropriate for an informal setting.

In general, it is better not to speak too formally. A speech should normally be in colloquial but correct style. Words and phrases belonging to written language, such as *inasmuch as* and *notwithstanding*, should be avoided. This is particularly true of words that explicitly refer to written texts, such as *the point mentioned above* or *in the previous section*.

If the speech is written out in full beforehand, there is a greater risk of sounding stuffy. To lessen the impression that a written speech is being read aloud, the following guidelines will help:

1. Keep the sentences short.
2. Formulate in a concise way.
3. Replace complicated words with more ordinary ones.
4. Vary the sentence structure (simple, complex) and the sentence type (declarative, interrogatory).
5. Use indicators of argumentation and standpoints (*because, therefore, firstly, in addition*) and conjunctions (*but, and*).
6. Use the passive form sparingly (instead of "In this speech a number of examples will be given ..." say "I will give a number of examples in this speech ...").
7. Illustrate abstract ideas or generalizations with concrete examples.
8. Address the audience directly from time to time ("Now you may ask yourselves ...").
9. Indicate clearly but in a natural-sounding way when you are going to quote someone (not by announcing "Here follows a quotation" but for example "as X once observed ...").
10. Give clear signals on where you are in your argument, and repeat important points.

Even a good speech can be spoiled by clumsy presentation. The time factor is often troublesome: The speech lasts way too long so that the speaker is forced to rush the last part of the speech. Such problems can be prevented by practicing the speech beforehand and timing it. Some other tips for a good presentation are:

1. Announce no more than what you are going to do.
2. Do not keep saying that there is much more to be said on the subject but that you do not have enough time to say it all.
3. Avoid giving an introduction to the introduction: "Before I begin my talk I first want to ..."
4. Avoid giving the impression that you are not well prepared or are indifferent to the subject. Do not say "On the way over here tonight I gave some thought to what I might say to you."
5. Do not be too critical of the audience or condescending. Do not explain things that everybody already knows. Do not say "For those of you who do not know what homeopathy is, I will explain ..." or "Of course you out in the country here don't keep up with all these developments ..."
6. Do not be overly modest and do not excuse yourself unnecessarily. Do not say "Unfortunately I don't know much about this topic, but ..." or "I know this isn't very important, but ..."

7. Do not keep postponing the conclusion. Do not say "In conclusion ..." or "The conclusion to be reached here is ..." unless you
   really are finishing up.
8. Instead of ending your speech suddenly, make sure you have a
   clearly identifiable conclusion. Do not put yourself in the position of ending by saying "Well, that's about it" or "I think I'll
   stop here."

FURTHER READING

A lot of useful advice concerning public speaking and debate can be
found in S. Beebe and S. J. Beebe, *Public Speaking: An Audience-centered
Approach* (4th ed.), Boston: Allyn & Bacon, 2000. Other prominent
American textbooks are M. Osborn and S. Osborn, *Public Speaking*,
Boston: Houghton Mifflin, 1988, and *The Elements of Public Speaking*
(4th ed.), New York: Harper & Row, 1990.

EXERCISES

1. Using the guidelines in this chapter, prepare an analytical overview for an argumentative speech, in which you
   —recommend a movie or a book
   —give your opinion on some current issue
   —make a suggestion for a change in the curriculum.
   Then give this speech to the class.

2. The following are the first paragraphs of a speech. Think of an introduction for this speech that would grasp the attention of the audience.

   Using animals as research subjects in medical investigations is widely condemned on two grounds: first, because it wrongly violates the rights of animals, and second, because it wrongly imposes on sentient creatures much avoidable suffering. Neither of these arguments is sound. The first relies on a mistaken understanding of rights; the second relies on a mistaken calculation of consequences. Both deserve definitive dismissal.

   Why animals have no rights? A right, properly understood, is a claim, or potential claim, that one party may exercise against another. The target against whom such a claim may be registered can be a single person, a group, a community, or (perhaps) all humankind. The content of rights claims also varies greatly: repayment of loans, nondiscrimination by employers, noninterference by the state, and so on. To comprehend any genuine right fully, therefore we must know who holds the right, against whom it is held, and to what it is a right.

SPECIAL ASSIGNMENT 8

a. Prepare a seven minute argumentative speech, starting from an analytical overview. Make use of the following format:
   1. Introduce the issue (topic, problem) you are going to discuss.
   2. Explain why this issue is interesting and/or important.
   3. State the position that you are going to defend.
   4. Discuss other positions.
   5. Present the arguments in favor of your position.
   6. Deal with counter-arguments.

      7. Summarize your case.

      8. End with a conclusion.

  b. Each student presents his/her speech in class. The speeches will be evaluated in the following way:

      1. All students in the audience fill in the evaluation form which is represented hereafter, and hand it back to the speaker.

      2. One student gives a short comment on the speech.

      3. The instructor comments on each speech.

EVALUATION FORM SPEECHES

Speaker:

Topic:

Date:

Quality and structure	**Grades:** **1 (very poor)–10 (excellent)**
Introduction of the issue (topic, problem)	---
Explanation of interest/importance issue	---
Statement of defended position	---
Discussion of other positions	---
Exposition of arguments in favor	---
Discussion of counter-arguments	---
Summary and conclusion of case	---
Balance and coherence between parts	---
Timing	---
Other comments	------------------------------------

Presentation and adaptation to audience	
Clarity of exposé	---
Concreteness (use of examples etc.)	---
Enthusiasm speaker	---
Arousing interest audience	---
Manner of speaking	---
Other comments	------------------------------------

Overview of Rules
For Critical Discussion
and Fallacies

RULES FOR CRITICAL DISCUSSION

1. Freedom rule

   Parties must not prevent each other from putting forward standpoints or casting doubt on standpoints.
2. Burden-of-proof rule

   A party who puts forward a standpoint is obliged to defend it if asked to do so.
3. Standpoint rule

   A party's attack on a standpoint must relate to the standpoint that has indeed been advanced by the other party.
4. Relevance rule

   A party may defend his or her standpoint only by advancing argumentation related to that standpoint.
5. Unexpressed premise rule

   A party may not falsely present something as a premise that has been left unexpressed by the other party or deny a premise that he or she has left implicit.

6. Starting point rule

   No party may falsely present a premise as an accepted starting point, or deny a premise representing an accepted starting point.

7. Argument scheme rule

   A standpoint may not be regarded as conclusively defended if the defense does not take place by means of an appropriate argument scheme that is correctly applied.

8. Validity rule

   The reasoning in the argumentation must be logically valid or must be capable of being made valid by making explicit one or more unexpressed premises.

9. Closure rule

   A failed defense of a standpoint must result in the protagonist retracting the standpoint, and a successful defense of a standpoint must result in the antagonist retracting his or her doubts.

10. Usage rule

    Parties must not use any formulations that are insufficiently clear or confusingly ambiguous, and they must interpret the formulations of the other party as carefully and accurately as possible.

FALLACIES

Violations of rule 1 (freedom rule) by the protagonist or the antagonist at the confrontation stage

1 *Placing limits on standpoints or doubts*
   - fallacy of declaring standpoints sacrosanct
   - fallacy of declaring standpoints taboo
2 *Restricting the other party's freedom of action*
   * putting the other party under pressure
   - fallacy of the stick (= argumentum ad baculum)
   - fallacy of appeal to pity (= argumentum ad misericordiam)
   * attacking the other party's person
     (= argumentum ad hominem)
   - fallacy of depicting the other party as stupid, bad, unreliable, etcetera (= direct personal attack/"abusive" variant)
   - fallacy of casting suspicion on the other party's motives
     (= indirect personal attack/"circumstantial" variant)
   - fallacy of pointing out a contradiction in the other party's words or deeds (= "tu quoque" variant)

Violations of rule 2 (burden-of-proof rule) by the protagonist at the opening stage

1   *Charging the burden of proof to the other party*
   * in a nonmixed difference of opinion, instead of defending his or her own standpoint the protagonist forces the antagonist to show that the protagonist's standpoint is wrong
   - fallacy of shifting the burden of proof
   * in a mixed difference of opinion the one party does not attempt to defend his or her standpoint but forces the other party to defend its standpoint
   - fallacy of shifting the burden of proof
2   *Escaping from the burden of proof*
   * presenting the standpoint as self-evident
   - fallacy of evading the burden of proof
   * giving a personal guarantee of the rightness of the standpoint
   - fallacy of evading the burden of proof
   * immunizing the standpoint against criticism
   - fallacy of evading the burden of proof

Violations of rule 3 (standpoint rule) by the protagonist or the antagonist at all the discussion stages

1   *Attributing a fictitious standpoint to the other party*
   * emphatically putting forward the opposite standpoint
   - fallacy of the straw man
   * referring to the views of the group to which the opponent belongs
   - fallacy of the straw man
   * creating a fictitious opponent
   - fallacy of the straw man
2   *Misrepresenting the other party's standpoint*
   * taking utterances out of context
   - fallacy of the straw man
   * oversimplifying or exaggerating
   - fallacy of the straw man

Violations of rule 4 (relevance rule) by the protagonist at the argumentation stage

1   *The argumentation has no relation to the standpoint under discussion*

- fallacy of irrelevant argumentation (= ignoratio elenchi)
2 *The standpoint is defended by means other than argumentation*
  * non-argumentation
  - fallacy of playing on the sentiments of the audience (= pathetic fallacy)
  - fallacy of parading one's own qualities (= ethical fallacy/abuse of authority)

Violations of rule 5 (unexpressed premise rule) by the protagonist or the antagonist at the argumentation stage

1 *Adding an unexpressed premise that goes beyond what is warranted*
  - fallacy of magnifying an unexpressed premise
2 *Refusing to accept commitment to an unexpressed premise implied by one's defense*
  - fallacy of denying an unexpressed premise

Violations of rule 6 (starting point rule) by the protagonist or the antagonist at the argumentation stage

1 *Meddling with the starting points by the protagonist by falsely denying that something is an accepted starting point*
  - fallacy of falsely denying an accepted starting point
2 *Meddling with the starting points by the antagonist by falsely presenting something as an accepted starting point*
  - fallacy of making unfair use of presuppositions in making assertions
  - fallacy of making unfair use of presuppositions in asking questions (= fallacy of many questions)
  - fallacy of using an argument that amounts to the same thing as the standpoint (= fallacy of circular reasoning/petitio principii/begging the question)

Violations of rule 7 (argument scheme rule) by the protagonist at the argumentation stage

1 *Using an inappropriate argument scheme*
  - populist fallacy (symptomatic relation) (= argumentum ad populum)
  - fallacy of confusing facts with value judgments (causal relation) (= argumentum ad consequentiam)
2 *Incorrectly applying an argument scheme*

- fallacy of authority (symptomatic relation) (= argumentum ad verecundiam)
- fallacy of hasty generalization (symptomatic relation) (= secundum quid)
- fallacy of false analogy (relation of analogy)
- fallacy of post hoc ergo propter hoc (causal relation)
- fallacy of the slippery slope (causal relation)

Violations of rule 8 (validity rule) by the protagonist at the argumentation stage

1   *Reasoning that treats a sufficient condition as a necessary condition*
    - fallacy of denying the antecedent
    - fallacy of affirming the consequent
2   *Reasoning that confuses the properties of parts and wholes*
    - fallacy of division
    - fallacy of composition

Violations of rule 9 (closure rule) by the protagonist or the antagonist at the concluding stage

1   *Meddling with the conclusion by the protagonist*
    - fallacy of refusing to retract a standpoint that has not been successfully defended
    - fallacy of concluding that a standpoint is true because it has been defended successfully
2   *Meddling with the conclusion by the antagonist*
    - fallacy of refusing to retract criticism of a standpoint that has been successfully defended
    - fallacy of concluding that a standpoint is true because the opposite has not been successfully defended (= argumentum ad ignorantiam)

Violations of rule 10 (usage rule) by the protagonist or the antagonist at all the discussion stages

1   *Misusing unclarity*
    - fallacy of unclarity (implicitness, indefiniteness, unfamiliarity, vagueness)
2   *Misusing ambiguity*
    - fallacy of ambiguity

General References

SURVEY OF ARGUMENTATION STUDIES

van Eemeren, F. H. (Ed.). (2001). *Crucial Concepts in Argumentation Theory.* Amsterdam: Amsterdam University Press.

van Eemeren, F. H., Grootendorst, R., Snoeck Henkemans, A. F., Blair, J. A., Johnson, R. H., Krabbe, E. C. W., Plantin, Ch., Walton, D. N., Willard, Ch. A., Woods, J., & Zarefsky, D. (1996). *Fundamentals of Argumentation: Theory. A Handbook of Historical Backgrounds and Contemporary Developments.* Mahwah, NJ: Lawrence Erlbaum Associates.

PRAGMA-DIALECTICAL THEORY OF ARGUMENTATION

van Eemeren, F. H., & Grootendorst, R. (1984). *Speech Acts in Argumentative Discussions. A Theoretical Model for the Analysis of Discussions Directed Towards Solving Conflicts of Opinion.* Dordrecht/Berlin: Foris/De Gruyter.

van Eemeren, F. H., & Grootendorst, R. (1992). *Argumentation, Communication, and Fallacies. A Pragma-Dialectical Perspective.* Hillsdale, NJ: Lawrence Erlbaum Associates.

van Eemeren, F. H., Grootendorst, R., Jackson, S., & Jacobs, S. (1993). *Reconstructing Argumentative Discourse.* Tuscaloosa-London: The University of Alabama Press.

van Eemeren, F. H., & Grootendorst, R. (Eds.). (1994). *Studies in Pragma-Dialectics.* Amsterdam: Sic Sat.

INTRODUCTION INTO FORMAL LOGIC

Kahane, H. (1987). *Logic and Philosophy: A Modern Introduction* (3rd ed.). Belmont, CA: Wadsworth.

SPEECH ACT THEORY AND RULES OF COMMUNICATION

Grice, P. (1989). *Studies in the Way of Words.* Cambridge. MA: Harvard University Press.

Searle, J. R. (1969). *Speech Acts. An Essay in the Philosophy of Language.* Cambridge, England: Cambridge University Press.

Searle, J. R. (1979). *Expression and Meaning: Studies in the Theory of Speech Acts.* Cambridge, England: Cambridge University Press.

Author Index

Subject Index